20.95

D1121808

# Death

*Other titles in the* Issues in Focus *series:*

Issues in Focus

# Death

## An Introduction to Medical-Ethical Dilemmas

Linda Jacobs Altman

**Enslow Publishers, Inc.**

40 Industrial Road        PO Box 38
Box 398               Aldershot
Berkeley Heights, NJ 07922   Hants GU12 6BP
USA                       UK

http://www.enslow.com

**Library of Congress Cataloging-in-Publication Data**

Altman, Linda Jacobs, 1943–
    Death: an introduction to medical-ethical dilemmas / Linda Jacobs
Altman.
      p.  cm. — (Issues in focus)
    Includes bibliographical references and index.
    Summary: Discusses issues surrounding death, including the stages
of death, prolonging life, euthanasia, religious and cultural views,
and funeral customs.
    ISBN 0-7660-1246-8
    1. Children and death—Juvenile literature.  2. Death—
Psychological aspects—Juvenile literature.  3. Death—Moral and
ethical aspects—Juvenile literature.  4. Euthanasia—Moral and
ethical aspects—Juvenile literature. [1. Death.]  I. Title. II. Series:
Issues in focus (Hillside, N.J.)
BF723.D3A57 2000
179.4—dc21                    99-32714
                                   CIP

Printed in the United States of America

10 9 8 7 6 5 4 3 2

**To Our Readers:**
All Internet addresses in this book were active and appropriate when we
went to press. Any comments or suggestions can be sent by e-mail to
Comments@enslow.com or to the address on the back cover.

**Illustration Credits:** Alexis Ciurczak, p. 6; Courtesy of the
Library of Congress, pp. 31, 55, 65, 75, 79, 81; Courtesy of
the U.S. National Library of Medicine, pp. 12, 16, 37, 42, 45,
50, 67, 84, 89, 91, 95; John F. Kennedy Library, p. 50.

**Cover Illustration:** Stock Market.

# Contents

In Mexico, the Day of the Dead is both a tribute to the dead and a festival for the living. People decorate the graves of the dead and create memorial offerings, called ofrendas, in their honor, which contain favored possessions of the deceased.

# 1

# The Way
# We Die

Teresa Hamilton lay still in her hospital bed, her small form all but hidden by life-support machinery. According to doctors at the Sarasota, Florida, hospital, the thirteen-year-old girl was dead. A ventilator kept her breathing, tubes kept her fed, a catheter eliminated her bodily wastes. But Teresa's brain was dead.

Three separate scans showed no brain activity at all. From a medical standpoint, the machines were not saving Teresa's life. They were only forcing automatic bodily functions to continue. The human being who had been Teresa Hamilton was already gone.

After more than a month of total life support, doctors asked to disconnect Teresa's equipment. Her parents said no. It was too early for such drastic action, they said. Teresa might yet recover. As long as her body functioned, they could hope for a miracle.

The doctors talked to the hospital ethics committee and the Florida attorney general. Both advised them to disconnect the system. The Hamiltons would not budge.

Six weeks after Teresa entered the hospital, the two sides reached a compromise. The hospital would send Teresa home, but keep her life-support equipment intact. A special ambulance took the teenager home shortly after the agreement was reached on February 18, 1994.[1]

She remained on life support for four months. On May 11, 1994, her heart collapsed, ending her young life completely. Her parents could no longer deny that she was dead.

There are no "good guys" and "bad guys" here. Teresa's parents were not trying to ruin the hospital's reputation. The doctors were not trying to murder a young girl. Teresa's story is a modern tragedy. It happened because medical technology is advancing beyond our ability to cope with the issues it raises.

It used to be that death was fairly straightforward. When a person stopped breathing and the heart stopped beating, life was over. Today, it is not so simple. We have a whole new set of issues surrounding death.

Technology can keep the heart and lungs going

even when the brain is dead, the body a pale shadow of what it used to be. Is a person in this condition alive or dead? Questions such as this continue to plague medical science.

## How the Body Dies

Death does not occur all at once, but in stages. Even after heartbeat, breathing, and brain activity stop, some cells keep functioning for a time. For example, people's hair and fingernails continue to grow.

The process of dying begins with interruption of oxygen flow. When the blood can no longer carry enough oxygen, the heart stops beating. Circulation stops. There is no breathing, no sign of brain activity. Cell death begins. This is what doctors call *clinical death*.

Before, and sometimes during, clinical death, there is a brief period called the *agonal phase*. According to Sherwin Nuland, surgeon and professor of medicine at Yale University, whose book, *How We Die: Reflections on Life's Final Chapter*, won the National Book Award, the dying person is not aware of these "death agonies." Most of what happens is due to muscle spasms rather than pain. There is often "a short series of great heaving gasps." Sometimes, the chest or shoulders will heave, or there will be "a brief agonal convulsion." This final burst of activity "merges into clinical death, and . . . the permanence of mortality."[2]

The length of the dying process depends on the cause of death. Dying can be long and slow for the patient with a degenerative (gradually worsening) illness such as cancer or acquired immune deficiency syndrome (AIDS). It can be brutally swift for the victim of an accident, violent assault, or epidemic disease.

## Dying Quickly

Doctors define sudden death as "unexpected death within a few hours of onset of symptoms in persons neither hospitalized nor homebound."[3] In our modern world, the most common cause of sudden death is heart seizure. It is triggered by the blocking of an artery leading to the heart.

When the heart muscle cannot get enough blood, it goes into spasms called *angina pectoris* (in Latin, *angina* is "choking" or "throttling"; *pectoris* refers to the chest). If the blockage lasts too long, the heart dies. According to Dr. Nuland, heart seizures cause 80 to 90 percent of sudden deaths.[4]

The term *sudden death* generally means swift death from natural causes. Death resulting from injuries or wounds is called traumatic death. Doctors classify these deaths as immediate, early, and late.

Immediate death occurs within minutes of the injury. More than half of such deaths result from massive injuries to the heart, brain, spinal cord, or a major blood vessel. Victims often die of their injuries before help can arrive.

In early death, the victim dies within hours, usually from injury to head, lungs, or abdominal organs. Here, there is a window of opportunity, a time during which treatment can save lives. As Dr. Nuland notes, "rapid transportation, well-trained trauma teams, and battle-ready emergency rooms make the critical difference."

Late death refers to situations in which the victim dies days, or even weeks, after the injury. Despite medical efforts, injured organs such as the lungs, kidneys, or liver begin to fail. There may be undetected internal bleeding.

In the past, more people died of communicable diseases (diseases that can be passed from one person to another) than of any other cause. They died young, they died fast, and they died hard.

Diseases such as cholera, yellow fever, and smallpox swept through whole populations. These diseases killed so many that the living scarcely had time or energy to bury the dead. During the fourteenth century, bubonic plague, or black death, as it came to be called, wiped out one third of the world's population.

Vaccines and antibiotic drugs greatly reduced the death rate from epidemic diseases. For a time, beginning in the 1950s, people believed that these mass killers would be conquered once and for all.

In 1967, the World Health Organization (WHO) began a global campaign to wipe out smallpox. This ancient disease had killed tens of millions during its long history. In the WHO campaign, about 250 million people were vaccinated for smallpox every year.[5] By 1977, smallpox had been eradicated all over the world.

It was a great triumph, but not the final victory. New and deadly germs began to appear. In 1967—the

*When the process of death was largely unknown, mythic images substituted for fact. Here, death is a skeleton, leading his unconquerable legions against defenseless humankind.*

same year that WHO began its campaign against smallpox—a strange virus struck workers at a medical research facility in Marburg, Germany. It was carried by the green monkeys from Africa that the laboratory used as experimental animals. This new life form became known as a filovirus because of its odd, threadlike shape. It was deadlier than anything the researchers had seen before. It caused a hemorrhagic fever that killed 30 percent of its victims.

The symptoms of hemorrhagic fever are truly terrible. As the filovirus takes hold, blood chemistry breaks down. The tiny capillaries all over the body begin oozing blood. The victim dies in agony, fevered, delirious, and bleeding from every pore.

Gastroenterologist Frank Ryan, a fellow of the

Royal College of Physicians in England, described the impact of Marburg in his book on emerging viruses, *Virus X: Tracking the New Killer Plagues—Out of the Present and Into the Future*:

> It is difficult for us today to realize what a shock the appearance of the Marburg virus created a generation ago. In 1967, the world of micro-biology took comfort in the conceit that most, if not all, new forms of infection were known. Now . . . a totally new life form had emerged from a rain forest [monkey] and hopped species to mount . . . [a deadly] attack on humanity.[6]

Nine years later, a new and even deadlier filovirus appeared. It was called *Ebola* after the African river where it was discovered. *Ebola* developed into two separate strains. *Ebola Sudan* killed 50 percent of its victims. *Ebola Zaire* had a terrifying 90 percent death rate.

## Dying Slowly

Not all emerging infections are swift killers. In the early 1980s, yet another new virus came out of Africa: the human immunodeficiency virus (HIV). This is the pathogen (harmful organism) that causes AIDS. It is a slow-acting virus that can copy itself directly into human cells. Unlike the filoviruses, HIV does not produce symptoms immediately. It can remain inactive for a long time, then flare into full-blown AIDS.

AIDS strips the body of its defenses against infection by slowly destroying the immune system. Victims get a host of rare infections, one after another. Finally, the body is overwhelmed and the victim dies.

In spite of the horrors of these new infections, life expectancy has continued to rise throughout the twentieth century. In 1900, life expectancy in the United States was 48.3 years for males, 51.1 for females; by 1996, those figures were up to 75.7 years for men, 82.7 for women.[7]

Today, people live long enough to die from slow killers such as heart disease, cancer, or one of the mind-robbing forms of dementia. With these degenerative diseases, medical advances have been a mixed blessing. Efforts to prolong life have too often led only to prolonging the process of dying.

In June 1998, a 103-year-old Sacramento, California, woman was brought into an emergency room with a heart attack. The doctor gave her morphine for the pain and set to work.

> Within four days, at least eight physicians were involved in her care. There were complications. The woman suffered heart failure and a drop in blood pressure. She was put on a ventilator. A minimum of seven intravenous lines were threaded through her veins. She became comatose (in a state of profound unconsciousness) and developed . . . pneumonia.[8]

Finally, the woman's heart failed. Once more, the doctors tried to revive her. This time they could not. On the fifth day of her hospitalization, the elderly patient died. At a seminar on medical ethics, some people argued that the woman should have been allowed to die right away. Others thought the doctors had acted correctly. Their job was to save lives with all the resources at their command.

This case brings up questions that plague everyone who grapples with issues of life and death in the bewildering world of high-tech medicine. How much is too much? When, if ever, should a patient simply be allowed to die?

## Death as the Enemy

Some of the conflicts over these questions may be traced to our modern attitude toward death. As Dr. Nuland puts it, our society tends to regard death as "a pitched battle that must be won."[9] No doctor likes to say, "There's nothing more I can do for this patient." That feels like giving up, like failure.

With modern technology, doctors are winning more life-and-death battles than at any other time in history. Unfortunately, that same technology makes it possible to win the battle while losing the war.

Life-support machines can sustain heartbeat and respiration almost indefinitely. This means that older definitions of death no longer make sense. In 1983, the President's Commission for the Study of Ethical Problems in Medicine adopted a new definition: "whole brain" death. When all brain activity ceases, the patient may be considered dead.

This definition does not cover all possible cases. Nowhere is this clearer than in what is called persistent vegetative state (PVS). In PVS, the conscious (thinking) brain dies, but the stem, which regulates automatic functions such as breathing and heartbeat, does not.

The case that brought the harsh reality of PVS to public attention was that of Karen Ann Quinlan. In April 1975, the twenty-one-year-old Quinlan lapsed into a coma. Just what happened to her is uncertain. On the night of her coma, Quinlan was apparently taking prescription medicines for menstrual cramps. She went out for dinner and drinks with a few friends.

Later that night, she became unconscious. An

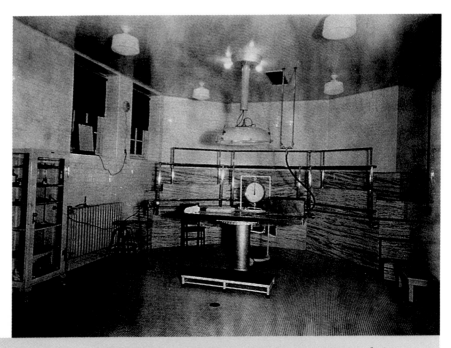

*An autopsy room at the Walter Reed Army Hospital in Washington, D.C. Autopsies are postmortem (after death) examinations conducted to determine the cause of death.*

ambulance took her to a nearby hospital, where she was placed on a respirator. Author Marilyn Webb described what happened after that:

> By the end of May, her limbs were becoming rigid, crimping, contorting farther into her chest. Her head started to flail sideways, back and forth, her neck craning backward as if her spine had broken. Soon, her body shrank smaller and smaller. Over the next few months . . . her body wound itself into a [twisted] three-foot-long fetal ball.[10]

The doctors and Quinlan's parents realized that there was no hope. After consulting the hospital chaplain and their own priest, Joe and Julia Quinlan asked to have their daughter's respirator disconnected. When the hospital refused, the Quinlans sued. That was the beginning of a long court fight—and a media circus.

On September 12, 1975, the Quinlan lawyer filed papers seeking the authority to turn off Karen Quinlan's respirator. The next day's headline read: "Father Seeks the Legal Right to Let His Gravely Ill Daughter Die."[11] Not until March 31, 1976, did the family win permission to remove "extraordinary treatments."[12]

The ruling immediately raised new questions. How should Quinlan be removed from the respirator? Slowly, to give her body chance to adjust, or suddenly? Did "extraordinary treatments" include the tubes that gave Quinlan food and water? Without them, she would quietly starve to death.

Neither the court nor the Quinlans dealt with the

issue of artificial nutrition. The feeding tube was left in place when the respirator was finally disconnected on May 22, 1976. Karen Quinlan did not die then, as everyone had expected. Her brain stem functioned on its own, keeping her in a void between life and death. She stayed that way for nearly ten years. Not until June 11, 1985, did Karen Ann Quinlan die, never having regained consciousness.

The Quinlan case triggered nationwide debate on end-of-life issues. The 1983 decision that set the "whole brain" standard grew out of that debate. Oddly enough, this new test would not have helped Karen Quinlan, since her brain stem functioned without artificial aid.

In 1985, another landmark ruling dealt with artificial nutrition and hydration. The New Jersey Supreme Court allowed doctors to remove the feeding tube of Claire Conroy, a comatose eighty-four-year-old woman.

Although this case helped to clarify a major issue, many others remain. Each new advance in medical technology seems to raise new and troubling questions. Amid all this controversy, one thing appears certain: For many years to come, our society will face hard choices about life, health, and the way we die.

# 2

# Facing the End

"Death," said Swiss-educated psychiatrist Elisabeth Kübler-Ross in her groundbreaking book, *On Death and Dying*, "has always been distasteful to man and will probably always be. . . . in our unconscious mind, we can only be killed; it is [unthinkable] to die of a natural cause or of old age."[1]

People with fatal illnesses must face this unthinkable event whether or not they are ready for it. A disease such as AIDS or inoperable cancer brings a person face-to-face with his or her own mortality. What happens then depends on the person, the illness, and the available treatments.

## New Answers, Old Questions

Prolonged dying raises many questions for doctors, patients, and families. Some people want to fight all the way. They will undergo every possible treatment, regardless of the cost or the suffering they must endure. Others draw a line in the sand; this far, and no farther. When they decide that further treatment is useless, they may seek palliative, or comfort, care.

It is at that line in the sand where we find the deepest conflicts. In order to draw it in the first place, the patient must admit that he or she is dying, and then make some hard decisions about end-of-life care. If the person can no longer make decisions, someone else must take the responsibility.

Medical professionals and other interested people have developed ethical guidelines for dealing with issues of death. They seek to define the time when the focus of treatment should change from cure to comfort care.

The guidelines offered by a California group called Extreme Care, Humane Options (ECHO) are typical. ECHO decided that comfort care should be offered when

- a patient is in a persistent vegetative state

- there is minimal [mental] function that is irreversible

- the burden to the patient of . . . treatment is greater than the medical benefit to the patient

- there is . . . [multi-]organ failure [that cannot be reversed or repaired]

- demise is imminent [death is about to happen][2]

These guidelines help patients and doctors come to grips with one all-important question: Can a prospective treatment do enough good to justify the suffering it may cause?

The answer will differ with every patient. Suppose, for example, that several weeks of painful radiation and chemotherapy could shrink a tumor enough to allow perhaps six months to a year of additional life. Some people would grab at that chance. Others might decide that the possibility of living a few months longer would not be worth the certainty of pain and suffering from the treatments.

## How People Really Die

Some doctors and medical ethicists believe we need a whole new vocabulary to talk meaningfully about dying. This new vocabulary should open choices rather than shut them down. It should acknowledge that death, however much we may dread it, is a natural part of the life process.

Dr. Nuland points out that ours is a death-denying society. We have trouble admitting that people can die simply because their bodies wear out:

> No one dies of old age, or so it would be . . . if [statisticians] ruled the world. . . . Everybody is required to die of a named [disease or injury]. . . . I have never [dared] to write "Old Age" on a death certificate, knowing that the form would be returned to me with a terse note . . . informing me that I had broken the law.[3]

In truth, human bodies do wear out. Nature designed them that way. If a person lives long enough, his or her body will shut down, organ by organ and function by function, until death occurs. Dr. Nuland argues that an elderly person's last illness is simply the final stage in that process, and he suggests that it be called the "terminal event" rather than the "cause of death."

"Cause" implies that a particular disease or injury killed the person. If not for the heart seizure or the automobile crash, he or she would still be alive. "Terminal event" implies that the final sickness or injury ended the life of a person whose body was already failing. This would bring descriptions of death in line with how it really occurs.

## Hope in the Face of Hopelessness

A realistic approach to death also includes dealing with hope, or the lack of it. Too often in our society, the fatally ill person has only one hope: the hope for a cure. When that hope becomes unrealistic, the patient has nothing left to ease the emotional pain of dying. Knowing this, many doctors are not entirely frank with their dying patients. They hold out hope where none exists.

The answer to this dilemma, says author Marilyn Webb, does not lie in comforting falsehoods:

> . . . in this age of seemingly ever-possible cures and chronic decline, when life may be prolonged nearly indefinitely, *hope* needs to be redefined. Today, hope for the dying is the hope for a good

death, however the person who is dying might define it.[4]

Hope may focus on the person's religious faith, or *Analysis* the desire to help loved ones prepare for his or her coming death. It may focus on the patient's desire to accomplish one last thing before dying, or the need to figure out the meaning of his or her own life.

For teenage AIDS patient Ryan White, hope lay in surviving longer than anyone thought he could and raising public awareness about the disease that was killing him.

In 1984, Ryan contracted AIDS from a blood transfusion. He suffered from hemophilia, a condition that prevents blood from clotting normally. Without frequent transfusions of clotting factors, hemophiliacs can bleed to death from the tiniest cut. With one of those transfusions, Ryan received blood contaminated with HIV, the virus that causes AIDS.

The doctors gave him six months to live, but Ryan White was a fighter. Not only did he survive for five years, he transformed public attitudes about people with AIDS.

AIDS was still new in 1984. People were terrified of anyone who was infected with the deadly virus. When Ryan's school banned him from classes, he sued for the right to return. A year later, the court ruled in Ryan's favor. The case made headlines all over the nation. Ryan became a living symbol of courage in the face of horror.

He died on April 8, 1990, at the age of eighteen. His legacy was the Ryan White CARE Act, which

Congress enacted to improve the quality of care for AIDS patients and their families. By holding on to hope in the face of certain death, Ryan White helped to make the world a better place for people afflicted with AIDS. In the process, he validated his own life.

## Defining Fatal Illness

Many who deal with the dying have called for new ways of categorizing fatal illnesses. Currently, *terminal illness* is a very narrow term, meaning that the person has less than six months to live. Under the rules of many insurance programs, only terminal patients can qualify for care in a hospice (an institution or program that specializes in end-of-life care).

This allows too many sick and suffering people to fall through the cracks of the health care system. Dr. Joanne Lynn of the Center to Improve Care of the Dying calls for a new and broader term: "life-defining, eventually fatal condition."[5]

With this approach, people suffering from degenerative diseases could receive comfort care sooner in the course of their illnesses. This would be of special benefit to victims of diseases such as Alzheimer's or amyotrophic lateral sclerosis (ALS or Lou Gehrig's disease). These diseases kill slowly. Doctors can rarely say when a particular patient can be considered terminal.

Typically, patients decline over time, until they need round-the-clock care months or even years before they die. The result is that many patients never qualify for programs that could ease their passing or help their families with the tremendous responsibilities of caretaking.

Dr. Lynn's classification would also benefit patients who want to continue fighting for their lives. Under current regulations, only those who abandon treatments aimed at curing their disease or prolonging their lives can qualify for hospice care. In other words, hospice is for people who have given up the fight for survival and resigned themselves to death.

Not all fatally ill people are willing to do this. Some want to stay alive as long as they can, perhaps in the hope that science will produce a cure before their time runs out. Dr. Lynn's classification is broad enough to allow these people to plan along two tracks: one, that they recover; the alternative, that they do not.[6]

## The High Cost of Survival

In this age of medical miracles, the hope for a timely cure is not unreasonable. Even HIV may be yielding to new treatments. Up until the mid-1990s, it was only a matter of time before HIV-positive patients developed full-blown AIDS.

In 1996, there was a breakthrough. Researchers developed a three-drug combination, or "cocktail" that reduced HIV to undetectable levels in the bloodstream. This opened the possibility for keeping the virus under permanent control. Other drugs have lessened the effects of AIDS itself, and prolonged the lives of people with the disease.

These experimental treatments are complicated

and costly. Patients must take fourteen to twenty pills a day, at different times and in different combinations. The cost for this treatment can run up to fifteen thousand dollars a year.[7]

Without insurance or some form of public aid, only the wealthy could afford the lifesaving drug cocktail, as that pill combination is known. This is true of many treatments and procedures in the world of high-tech medicine. In the last two decades of the twentieth century, medical costs soared. The insurance industry responded with "managed care." In this system, also known as the gatekeeper approach, a person's primary physician is in charge of all care, and the physician decides whether or not to make referrals. In traditional health care plans, the insured consumer is free to choose whichever doctor he or she wishes to see.

Managed care is a hot topic. Insurance executives talk about it in their offices. Members of Congress debate it on Capitol Hill. News reporters write countless stories about the health care crisis in America. We cannot analyze this important issue in the space of a short book. The best we can do is to sketch in the broad outlines of managed care as it relates to life-or-death decisions.

At its best, managed care cuts medical costs by eliminating unnecessary tests, treatments, and medicines. At its worst, it puts a dollar value on human life. How do insurance companies decide that Patient A can have the new heart medicine that costs over two thousand dollars a dose, while Patient B cannot have it? Questions such as this are at the heart of the managed care controversy.

## The Dilemma of Transplant Surgery

When a treatment is not only expensive, but scarce, the questions become even more complex. Organ transplants are a good example. Not everyone who needs a transplant will get it. Some candidates will not be accepted on a waiting list. Some will be on a list, only to die before a suitable organ can be found for them.

Waiting lists do not work on a "first come, first served" basis. When an organ becomes available, it is not necessarily the sickest person who gets it. Organ and patient must be matched by blood group and other factors. Some people may be on a list for months or even years, while others are matched almost immediately.

The selection process for organ transplants has become a topic of controversy. In 1995, the case of baseball great Mickey Mantle caused a widespread public outcry. Mantle's liver was damaged by long-term alcoholism and finally destroyed by cancer. Although his general physical health was poor, he was placed on a transplant list and received a new liver within two days. He died a few months later, of cancer that had spread through his body and destroyed the transplanted liver.

Did Mickey Mantle receive special treatment because he was famous? Would an ordinary person in his condition have even been placed on the list?

These were the questions debated on television and in the newspapers. The doctors who performed the operation denied any favoritism. Mantle was on the list because they believed a transplant could save his life. He received the operation so quickly because he was the best match for that particular liver.

In deciding who is a good candidate for transplant surgery, doctors take many factors into account. Among these factors are the patient's age, general health, and ability to deal with lifelong aftercare. Transplant patients must take powerful drugs to prevent their bodies from rejecting the new organ. The drugs are expensive, the medication schedule is complex, and mistakes can be fatal.

Sandra Jensen of Sacramento, California, was turned down for two waiting lists because she had Down syndrome, a form of mental retardation. Jensen, whose heart and lungs were failing, protested that she was being discriminated against because of her disability.

Despite her Down syndrome, she had graduated from high school. She lived in her own apartment and held a steady job, working in a cafeteria. She was also an outspoken advocate for the rights of the disabled.

Friends, relatives, and civil rights advocates rallied to Jensen's cause. In January 1996, doctors at the Stanford University Medical Center performed the difficult double transplant. Sandra Jensen became the first person with Down syndrome to have the operation. She managed her aftercare well, properly taking each medication at the right time and reporting for follow-up visits on schedule.

Fourteen months after her surgery, Sandra Jensen died from complications of the antirejection drugs: "This was a complication that can occur with anyone who has a transplant," her doctor said. "I want to emphasize that it had nothing to do with her as a person, or as someone with Down syndrome."[8]

Jensen lived long enough to know that her struggle had made a difference. The California state legislature passed a law preventing doctors and hospitals from denying transplants solely on the basis of a person's disability.

## Coming to Terms with Death

In 1969, Dr. Elisabeth Kübler-Ross published *On Death and Dying*. The book would help to change the way our society thinks about death. Dr. Kübler-Ross saw how the dying got trapped in a medical system that did not quite know what to do with them. Too many people were spending their last days surrounded by monitors, tubes, and strangers. What did these people think? What did they want and need? Dr. Kübler-Ross decided to find out.

She invited dying patients to meet with her medical students. Each patient would tell the group about his or her experiences, feelings, and needs. At first, students were timid about discussing death with somebody who was actually dying. In time, this changed and the interviews became remarkably open and frank.

From these interviews, Dr. Kübler-Ross identified five stages of the dying process: denial, anger, bargaining, depression, and acceptance. Although there is a rough sequence to these stages, there is also a great deal of overlapping. People tend to shift back and forth: now accepting, now denying, now becoming depressed or angry. Some die without ever having reached acceptance.

Each stage has its own typical behaviors. In denial, patients simply refuse to believe they can be dying. They think the diagnosis must be wrong, or perhaps the laboratory got the test results mixed up.

With time, most patients face the truth. Then the anger begins, anger at God for allowing such a terrible thing to happen, anger at family, friends, and medical personnel. Anger at life itself.

When the anger has spent itself, people start to bargain. Often this is a delaying tactic. "If only I had life and strength enough to . . ." The last part of that statement is different for everyone. It may range from attending one last class reunion to "seeing Paris once before I die," or completing an important project.

Dr. Kübler-Ross tells of a cancer patient who was in terrible pain. She wanted nothing so much as to attend her oldest son's wedding:

> [We] were able to teach her self-hypnosis, which enabled her to be quite comfortable for several hours. She had made all sorts of promises if only she could live long enough to attend this marriage. The day [before] the wedding she left the hospital as an elegant lady. Nobody would have believed her real condition. She was "the happiest person

*Parents face the death of a frightened child with bleak resignation and sadness, in this painting by Käthe Kollwitz (1867–1945).*

in the whole world" and looked radiant. . . . I'll never forget the moment when she returned to the hospital. She looked tired and somewhat exhausted and—before I could say hello—said, "Now don't forget I have another son!"[9]

When patients quit bargaining, they often sink into deep depression. Some patients focus on events they can no longer control. Others are grieving for the life that is about to end.

For the first type of depression, Dr. Kübler-Ross uses the example of a mother worrying about leaving her children: "It may help a mother to know that [the children] continue to laugh and joke, go to parties, and bring good report cards home from school—all expressions that they function in spite of mother's absence."[10]

The second type of depression is "a tool to prepare for the [coming] loss. . . . The patient is in the process of losing everything and everybody he loves. If he is allowed to express his sorrow, he will find a final acceptance much easier."[11]

This acceptance is rarely happy or even contented, but it can be serene. The patient quietly begins the process of withdrawing from life. He or she eats less or not at all, sleeps more, and loses interest in the outside world. "It is as if the pain had gone, the struggle is over and there comes a time for 'the final rest before the long journey,'" as one patient of Dr. Kübler-Ross phrased it.[12]

## The Hospice Alternative

The work of Dr. Kübler-Ross, and that of Cicely Saunders, a British doctor, became the foundation for the modern hospice movement. Dr. Saunders became interested in care for the dying as a nursing student during World War II. After the war, she earned a degree in social work, followed by one in medicine.

In 1967, she founded St. Christopher's, a hospice in London. Her goal was to provide comfort care for the dying, along with emotional and psychological support. Many of St. Christopher's patients had forms of cancer that produced constant and unendurable pain. To help them, Dr. Saunders made pain control her first priority.

She used the "Brompton Cocktail," named for the British hospital where it was created. The Brompton mixture includes morphine, cocaine, alcohol, and antinausea medication. Most of these drugs are addictive, but that hardly seemed important for people with only weeks or months left to live. Dr. Saunders pioneered the practice of giving pain medication in steady doses around the clock. This shifted the emphasis from pain relief to pain prevention.

The first hospice in the United States was founded by Florence Wald in 1974. Wald, dean of the Yale University School of Nursing, set up Connecticut Hospice as an outpatient program. A staff of doctors, nurses, counselors, and home aides provided support for the dying patient and his or her caregivers.

This focus on home care has continued in the American hospice movement. Many programs do operate a small inpatient facility for patients without home care. Others contract with local hospitals to set aside rooms for comfort care patients.

A good hospice is able to deal with many different illnesses. A 1995 survey by the National Hospice Organization showed that "60 percent of hospice patients had cancer, 6 percent had heart-related ailments, 6 percent had AIDS, Alzheimer's, or kidney-related diagnoses, and 20 percent had 'other' illnesses."[13]

Whatever the illness, patients are in control of treatment. Dr. Judith C. Ahronheim writes:

> An important [part] of palliative care is avoiding unwanted high-tech treatments that can prolong dying and produce pain or discomfort. Patients have the right to decide whether they want these treatments. They also have the right to stop such treatments after they have been started. Discontinuing a painful treatment almost always reduces discomfort. If . . . the person still is experiencing discomfort, pain medications or sedatives are given.[14]

In 1996, Dr. Ira Byock founded a model hospice program in Missoula, Montana. The Quality of Life's End Missoula Demonstration Project is not just a research project. It is a working hospice, on the cutting edge of end-of-life care. Patients are encouraged to record a lifetime of stories: Things they did, places they went, people they knew. These stories run the gamut of human experience. They can be happy, sad, sweet, bitter, funny, or downright outrageous. Sharing their stories helps patients explore the meaning of their own lives and creates a legacy of memories to leave behind.

## Legal Issues at the End of Life

Healthy people do not like to think about dying. Death is a fact of life. We all know that, but most of us would just as soon ignore it as long as possible.

For those who want control of their own lives to the very end, ignoring issues of death is not a good idea. It may place decisions into the hands of strangers who do not understand the patient's wishes, needs, or ethical values. It can mean unwanted treatments, family conflicts, even bitter legal battles.

Advance directives set forth the patient's desires about health care. They do not take effect unless the patient is incapable of making his or her own decisions. According to the American Academy of Family Physicians, a good advance directive

> describes the kind of treatment you would want to receive for different levels of illness. For example, the directives would describe what kind of care you would want if you have a critical illness, a terminal illness or permanent unconsciousness.[15]

Living wills are a particular type of advance directive. They only become effective when the patient is terminally ill and cannot make his or her own decisions. The living will specifies the care a person wants or does not want under these conditions. A sample living will from the American Association of Retired Persons shows typical clauses:

> DIRECTIVE TO WITHHOLD OR WITHDRAW TREATMENT. Although I greatly value life, I also believe that at some point, life has such diminished value that medical treatment should be

stopped, and I should be allowed to die. Therefore, I do not want to receive treatment, including nutrition and hydration, when the treatment will not give me a meaningful quality of life . . .[16]

The clause goes on to discuss circumstances such as irreversible coma, loss of mental function, and situations where "the likely risks and burdens of treatment outweigh the expected benefits."[17] These risks and benefits include "length of life, quality of life, financial costs, and my personal dignity and privacy."[18]

For those who do not want treatment stopped, the sample living will makes a clear statement of that fact: "DIRECTIVE TO RECEIVE TREATMENT. I want my life to be prolonged as long as possible, no matter what my quality of life."[19]

A durable power of attorney (DPA) for health care allows an individual to choose an agent (usually a close relative), who will make health care decisions on his or her behalf. The DPA is not limited to end-of-life treatment. It goes into effect any time the individual is unconscious or otherwise unable to make decisions.

The do-not-resuscitate (revive) order is the simplest kind of advance directive. It is a doctor's order, placed into a hospital chart at the patient's request. It tells hospital staff not to revive the patient if his or her heartbeat or respiration should stop.

Advance directives are meant to reduce suffering for people whose chances of recovery or meaningful life are low. They represent progress in dealing with

*In this sixteenth century engraving, an elderly man meets death in the presence of his family and friends, who grieve at losing him.*

the unintended consequences of high-tech medicine. Unfortunately, they do not answer all the questions about end-of-life care. Tough issues remain.

Professional societies, governmental agencies, and patient rights groups continue to sort through those issues. Their goal is to find answers that respect the sanctity of life while acknowledging the inevitability of death.

# 3

# Choosing Death

On June 1, 1990, Janet Adkins, her husband, Ron, and her best friend Carroll Rehmle flew from Portland, Oregon, to Detroit, Michigan. Ron and Carroll were going there to be with her. Janet Adkins was going there to die.

The fifty-four-year-old music teacher planned to kill herself with the help of Dr. Jack Kevorkian. Kevorkian became known as "Doctor Death" for his stand on assisted suicide. Adkins was his first patient.

## Janet Adkins's Choice

Adkins did not take this action without a great deal of thought. About a year earlier,

38

she had gone to see her doctor about some disturbing symptoms. She was forgetting things—not just where she put the car keys or the name of a new acquaintance, but basic things. She would sit down to play the piano and find she could not decipher the music. She could not balance a checkbook or read a credit card statement. She could still play tennis, but she could not determine the score.

After a series of tests, the doctor told her the bad news: She had Alzheimer's disease. Her memory would slowly fail. In time, she would not recognize her own family and friends. She would need help with the simplest tasks of daily living, from going to the bathroom to getting dressed. Eventually, her body would "forget" how to function, her system would shut down, and she would die.

"I want an exit,"[1] Janet Adkins said, right after the diagnosis. Her husband, Ron Adkins, was stunned by this announcement, but not entirely surprised. As longtime members of the Hemlock Society, he and Janet had considered these issues before. The Society believes that terminally ill people should have the right to choose the manner and the time of *suicide* their own deaths. Janet believed she would be affirming her life by ending it on her own terms.

Still, she did not immediately start looking for ways to die or for people to help her do it. Accepting the idea of choice about dying was one thing. Actually deciding to kill herself was quite another.

Before going to Dr. Kevorkian, Janet went through counseling with her husband and three grown sons. She agreed to try an experimental drug program at the University of Washington. When her condition did not improve after ten weeks of treatment, she had run out of options. She contacted Dr. Kevorkian.

On June 4, 1990, Adkins kept her appointment with Dr. Kevorkian. They met in the back of a Volkswagen van, which was the only place available for this grim procedure. Dr. Kevorkian had tried to find a more suitable place. He checked doctors' offices, hotels, and friends' houses. He even tried to rent an ambulance. Everybody turned him down.

So it was that Janet Adkins ended up in a rusty white van, parked on an isolated campground. She sat quietly while Dr. Kevorkian hooked her up to his "suicide machine."[2]

He had created the device out of scrap aluminum and parts of a toy car. It would allow the patient herself to push the button that would release the lethal drugs into her body. In this way, Dr. Kevorkian could truthfully state that Janet Adkins had died by her own hand.

Dr. Kevorkian put a needle into Janet's arm and started a harmless saline (salt) solution. All Janet had to do was push a button to release an anesthetic that would put her to sleep. A solution of potassium chloride would follow automatically, stopping her heart.

When it was over, Dr. Kevorkian made two phone calls. One was to Ron Adkins, to tell him that Janet was dead. The other was to the police to report what he had done. Dr. Kevorkian was later charged with murder, but the judge threw the case out of court for lack of evidence. The battle over mercy killing had begun.

## The Language of Deliberate Death

The struggle over right-to-die issues has created a new vocabulary of death. *Euthanasia*, for example, is an ancient Greek word that literally means "good death." In modern terminology, it has come to mean "mercy killing," or "causing painless death, particularly in those suffering from incurable, painful diseases."[3] A dying AIDS patient once called it "an act of God performed by mortals."[4]

In euthanasia, a doctor or other caretaker directly causes the death of a patient. When the patient has requested this action, the euthanasia is considered voluntary. When he or she has not made such a request, it is involuntary.

Indirect euthanasia, sometimes called terminal sedation, refers to giving large doses of sedatives to bring about unconsciousness. When a dying patient is suffering unbearable pain, terminal sedation is considered acceptable medical practice.

The word *suicide* has also been modified in the debate about right-to-die issues. Suicide is the deliberate ending of one's own life. It becomes assisted suicide when someone else provides the means for the act of self-killing. When that someone else is a doctor, it is physician-assisted suicide.

*Silent suicide* is a term often used to describe self-starvation. This practice is most often used in extreme old age. The person simply quits eating and refuses to accept artificial nutrition or hydration.

## Motives for Suicide

Right-to-die advocates distinguish between rational and irrational suicide. Rational suicide results from a decision made by a person who faces a painful or dehumanizing death from an incurable disease. Irrational suicide results from depression, anger, fear, or an emotional disorder.

Under these definitions, Janet Adkins's suicide would be considered rational. The suicide of fifteen-year-old Brandy Harris would not. Brandy was not

*In this etching entitled "The Blue Devils," a despondent man contemplates suicide. His thoughts are represented by demons that plague him with images of failure and death.*

suffering from a terminal illness. She was young, depressed, and frightened. Her troubled past included drugs, alcohol, and treatment for sexual abuse.

On January 21, 1996, Brandy Harris got hold of a gun and killed herself. Her family and friends were numb with grief. Irrational suicide, particularly of a young person, often haunts the survivors in a way that rational suicide does not. Family and friends are left to wonder if something they said or did pushed the victim over the edge.

Brandy's mother, Kathleen Bartlett, was determined to salvage some meaning from her daughter's life and death. She did this by donating Brandy's organs for transplants. Four people got a new chance at life because of that donation. One of them was Sandra Jensen, who made history as the first person with Down syndrome to receive transplant surgery.

Kathleen Bartlett saw a certain justice in this. Brandy was a fighter, she said. The fact that she lost her battle did not change that. Sandra Jensen was also a fighter. "What better person . . . to get Brandy's organs?"[5] Bartlett said. To her way of thinking, it was a perfect match.

## The Controversy Over Intentional Death

After the words are defined, we are still left with more questions than answers about intentional death. We are also left with a painful reality: For people dying from incurable disease, there comes a time when all the treatments in the medical arsenal become useless.

The old-time country doctor who put away his

medical bag to sit quietly beside a dying patient knew this. So does the modern oncologist who orders terminal sedation to ease the last hours of life.

The doctor who takes a more active role in helping a patient to die knows it all too well. Deliberate killing raises ethical and moral issues that can overshadow the fate of a single, suffering patient.

Coping with these issues will be a long, slow process. There are many possible positions on the subject of medically assisted dying. Some people want to legalize both assisted suicide and euthanasia. Others believe that helping a dying patient end his or her own life would be morally acceptable, but directly killing that same patient would be wrong. Still others claim that it does not matter who does the killing. Either way, human beings have claimed a power that does not rightfully belong to them.

Many people who take this last position have religious reasons. They believe that the power of life and death belongs only to God. Others fear that legalized killing will cheapen human life and set a dangerous standard for our whole society.

## *Final Exit*: The Work of Derek Humphry

The Hemlock Society is one of the best known of the right-to-die groups. It was founded by British-born journalist Derek Humphry. He became an advocate of euthanasia when his wife was dying of bone cancer.

When her pain became unbearable, Jean Humphry begged her husband to help her die. He did

*A young man courts death, which he envisions as a beautiful and desirable young woman.*

as she asked. Later, he wrote a book, *Jean's Way*, in which he told about the experience. It was first published in England and later, in the United States.

After the American publication, people began contacting Humphry for help. In response, he founded the Hemlock Society. Its purpose was to campaign for changes in laws regarding medically assisted dying.

Humphry knew it would take a long time to make these changes. What about people who were dying in the meantime? For them, he wrote another book. *Final Exit: The Practicalities of Self-Deliverance and Assisted Suicide for the Dying* told terminally ill people exactly how to go about killing themselves in the most painless way possible. Some called the book a blessing. Others called it a scandal.

Even doctors who wanted to legalize medically assisted dying criticized Derek Humphry's "ill-advised cookbook of death,"[6] as Dr. Nuland called it.

Humphry never stopped believing that publishing the book was the right thing to do. In support of this position, he cited the case of a ninety-year-old man who asked for help in committing suicide. "I advised him to read *Final Exit*, which he did and he called me back. He had gotten lethal drugs from a friendly doctor and so everything was in position.

'So what are you going to do now?' I asked him.

'Oh, I'm not ready to go yet,' he replied. 'I've got the means, so I can hold on a bit longer.'"[7]

Dr. Timothy Quill criticized Humphry's book for skimming over deep moral and ethical issues. Quill spoke from experience. He was once prosecuted (but not convicted) for prescribing lethal drugs for a terminally ill patient. He favored a more cautious approach to the issues. Quill said,

> I will be working . . . with the AMA [American Medical Association] and the American College of Physicians in the areas of heavy sedation and stopping eating and drinking. If we can allow that, that's going to be a big step in the right direction. Those changes don't require changes in the law. Changing the law is hard. . . . I think there will be activity there, but I'm less enthusiastic about that.[8]

## The Oregon Experiment

In 1994, Oregon voters passed America's first assisted suicide law. The Death With Dignity Act, as it was called, appeared as Measure 16 on the Oregon ballot. It allowed doctors to prescribe lethal drugs for mentally competent adults with less than six months to live.

Measure 16 squeaked by with 51 percent of the vote, but it still made history. All over the country, it triggered headlines and heated debates. People took sides on what promised to be "the most controversial medical issue of the 1990s."[9]

In Oregon, opponents moved to stop the law from taking effect. They kept it tied up in the courts for three years. Then they convinced the state legislature to send the measure back to the voters.

An initiative to repeal Measure 16 went on the ballot in November 1997. The Catholic Church and the National Right to Life Committee led the campaign for repeal. The effort did not work; Oregon voters affirmed physician-assisted suicide by an overwhelming 60 percent majority.

Barbara Coombs Lee, one of the original authors of Measure 16, called the victory "a turning point for the death-with-dignity movement."[10]

For sixty-six-year-old Barbara Oskamp, who had an inoperable brain tumor, the victory was not about social movements or medical ethics. It was far more personal than that. Oskamp stated,

> I don't know that I would be in bad pain at the end; obviously, I hope not. But it's the choice of having the pills up there on the bedside table. I don't know what I'd do. I don't know what I'd choose, but just the fact of having the pills there gives me a little relief.[11]

Measure 16 did not trigger a stampede by terminally ill people seeking to end their lives. In the first year, only eight people killed themselves with drugs legally prescribed by a doctor. Two others went through the screening procedure to get the drugs, but did not use them.

The first publicized case was that of a breast cancer victim in her mid-eighties. The woman, whose name was not released to the media, took a lethal dose of barbiturates on March 24, 1998. Her doctor and her family were with her to the end.

"I am deeply saddened at this news," said Archbishop John Vlazny of Portland. "The suicide of this elderly woman can only bring anguish to those who have resisted the . . . public policy initiatives that changed the law in Oregon."[12]

## The Slippery Slope

Opponents of assisted dying feared that the Oregon law would be a first step down the dreaded "slippery slope." The image of the slippery slope expresses a grim idea. An action that may not be immoral in itself can lead to other actions that violate our most cherished values.

The slippery slope might begin with a redefinition of the word *terminal*. There are already those who say that the right to die should not be limited to those who are terminally ill. What about people with fatal diseases of decline, such as Alzheimer's or ALS? Should they be forced to endure a hard and slow death if they choose instead to die?

Janet Adkins, for example, might have lived for many years, with Alzheimer's disease slowly robbing her of all the joyful aspects of life. Many people can understand how this particular woman in this particular situation could choose to die. But making the leap from personal decision to public policy is another matter—a much more difficult matter.

Already, some right-to-die activists are calling for broader laws. For them, Oregon's Death With Dignity Act was just a beginning. Derek Humphry has said that when "we have laws on the statute books that permit physician-assisted dying for the terminally ill . . . along with this reform will develop a more tolerant response" to the other exceptional cases.[13]

The "exceptional cases" Humphry is talking about are quadriplegics (people who are paralyzed from the neck down) and others with severe disabilities.

Humphry is careful to state that he means only those disabled people who want to end their lives and who are competent to make that decision. He also states clearly that he is talking about changes in attitude, not law.

Still, his call for wider acceptance of suicide implies that reforms in one area could lead to changes in another. It might begin with people who have less than six months to live. From there, it could expand to people with long-term degenerative diseases. Next might come those with nonfatal

*Although he was an internationally famous, well-respected writer, the American novelist Ernest Hemingway suffered from depression all his life. On July 2, 1961, only a few weeks before his sixty-second birthday, Hemingway committed suicide.*

disabilities who simply do not want to live with their handicaps. Where does it end? To opponents of assisted suicide, this is the critical question.

## The Spectre of Medical Killing

The ultimate example of the slippery slope is Nazi Germany in the 1930s and 1940s. Under the guise of what they called "euthanasia," Nazi doctors carried out a systematic program of murder. Their goal was to eliminate "inferior" people from the German Reich.

In his book, *Nazi Doctors*, Robert Jay Lifton discussed this "medicalized killing," as he called it.

> In Nazi mass murder, we can say that a barrier was removed, a boundary crossed . . . the medicalization of killing—the imagery of killing in the name of healing—was crucial to that terrible step. At the heart of the Nazi enterprise, then, is the destruction of the boundary between healing and killing.[14]

That destruction began slowly and advanced step by careful step. First came the forced sterilization of people with inherited defects. Next came the killing of deformed or mentally handicapped newborns. From there, the program expanded to include institutionalized children of all ages.

Mentally ill adults came next. It is estimated that at least 80,000 to 100,000 adult mental patients and 5,000 institutionalized children were killed under the supervision of doctors.[15]

The final horror was the Holocaust, the name given to the slaughter of six million Jews and about five million other "undesirables." These people were not sick or disabled. They simply did not fit into the Nazi vision of a master race.

In November 1998, Dr. Kevorkian stunned right-to-die activists with a videotape that showed him killing Thomas Youk, a fifty-two-year-old victim of ALS. The tape clearly showed the entire process, from Dr. Kevorkian giving the fatal injection to the actual death of the patient.

By giving the lethal agent himself, Dr. Kevorkian crossed the border between assisted suicide and euthanasia. "We need active euthanasia," he argued. "There are patients who just can't do this for themselves. From now on I'm doing them all that way—it is faster, cleaner and easier."[16]

Medical examiner Dr. L. J. Dragovic confirmed that Youk would "have been physically incapable of injecting himself."[17] In spite of this, Youk's death provoked a general outcry. Even right-to-die leaders moved quickly to censure Dr. Kevorkian. Barbara Coombs Lee made a forthright statement to the press: "What he's doing bears no relationship to our cause or what we stand for. He's as extreme as anyone can imagine. The very modest, moderate practice that is going on in Oregon couldn't be further away from this outrageous activity."[18]

Dr. Kevorkian's own lawyers disavowed his actions. Legal experts said he was flirting with a murder conviction.

They were right.

On April 14, 1999, Dr. Kevorkian was sentenced to ten to twenty-five years in the murder of Youk.[19]

Opponents of assisted dying were horrified. Dr.

Kevorkian's action seemed to confirm their worst fears. This time, he was not just standing at the top of the slippery slope. He had plunged headlong down the incline.

The reality of dealing with a patient's dying "is very different from its portrayal by Dr. Kevorkian," wrote Dr. Jerome Groopman in his book, *The Measure of Our Days: New Beginnings at Life's End*:

> The medical profession has its codes for easing the dying person's passage: "Expedite the process"; "Help nature take its course"; "Palliate maximally." Each aims to mask the stark reality of the act. . . . When the decision [to discontinue treatment] is made, I order the intensive life support withdrawn, and, if there is pain, an infusion of morphine begun. As I watch the breathing quiet, the flesh slowly cool, I am invariably seized by a sharp moment of doubt. Has everything been done that could have been done? Was there really no longer any reason to live? My fallibility [capacity for making mistakes] is never [clearer] to me than at that moment.[20]

Many other doctors would agree with Dr. Groopman. Perhaps some form of assisted dying should become legal, but it should never become routine. Deciding to help a patient die should be a struggle. It should mean sleepless nights and secret doubts. The very difficulty of the decision-making process is a safeguard against taking that first, fateful step down the slippery slope.

# 4

# Saying Goodbye

Every society has rites of passage to mark the important moments of life: birth, coming-of-age, marriage, parenthood, and of course, death. Ritual and time-honored custom surround the dying process from deathbed to tomb, and even beyond. These observances ease the dying person's passage, honor the life that he or she has led, and comfort those left behind to mourn.

Some customs are solemn and dignified. Others are filled with outbreaks of raw emotion. A few are downright outrageous. For example, the mobster funerals of Chicago in the 1920s became famous for their showy and costly displays.

On November 10, 1924, gangster Dion O'Banion was shot to death by gunmen from a rival mob. O'Banion himself was little noted outside the Chicago criminal community. His funeral made him a national celebrity. It was a magnificent affair, worthy of kings, princes, and heads of state. The casket alone was said to cost $10,000, a princely sum in 1924.[1]

The funeral procession was a mile long, with ten

*Pomp and splendor usually surround the funerals of prominent people. The coffin of President Abraham Lincoln is displayed, surrounded by floral displays.*

thousand mourners, three marching bands, twelve limousines loaded with floral displays, and a police escort. Another ten thousand people waited at the gravesite.

Al Capone and Johnny Torrio, the mobsters who ordered the "hit" on O'Banion, were among the mourners. They looked appropriately grief-stricken as they listened to the eulogies for their "friend."

## The Deathbed Vigil

When a person lies dying, it is often the custom for family members to keep vigil at the bedside. Their presence is supposed to validate the person's life, and ease his or her passing. The one who is dying also has a role to perform. If able, he or she makes final bequests and generally ties up the loose ends of the life that is about to end.

In *On Death and Dying*, Dr. Kübler-Ross recalled the deathbed actions of a farmer who had lived near the doctor's childhood home:

> He called his daughters into the bedroom and spoke with each one of them alone for a few minutes. He arranged his affairs quietly, though he was in great pain, and distributed his belongings and his land. . . . He also asked each of his children to share in the work, duties, and tasks that he had carried on until the time of the accident. He asked his friends to visit him once more, to bid goodbye to them.[2]

In addition to setting worldly affairs in order, the dying person attends to spiritual matters. Catholics make their last confession to a priest and receive the sacrament of extreme unction to prepare the soul for the spiritual world. Jews are supposed to say the prayer *Shema* ("Hear O Israel, the Lord is our God, the Lord is One") with their last breath.

Last words are important. They have ranged from outright wisecracks to pious pronouncements. Some have been sorrowful, some brave, some wistful. The last words of French writer Francois Rabelaise (1494–1553) are said to have been, "I am going now to seek for a great perhaps."[3]

It is not the content of last words that makes them important. It is their finality. Last words are the ultimate exit line, so whatever the dying person says will be remembered. Mexican revolutionary leader Pancho Villa knew this as well as anyone. His last words were "Don't let it end like this. Tell them I said something clever."[4]

In the 1990s, the video camera brought a new dimension to the deathbed statement—the farewell video. Videos seem to have become a part of all our rites of passage, transforming everything from birthdays to bar mitzvahs and even childbirth into photo opportunities. It is as if these occasions are not "real" without a videotape record.

British anthropologist Nigel Barley notes that most of these videos are "sickly-sweet and maundering [wandering; foolish], dwelling on love and support given, the eyes morphine-crazed, the smile rigid and fixed, the words as pointless and trite as the obligatory holiday postcard."[5]

## Preparing the Body

The period between death and burial or cremation (burning of the body) has its own set of rituals. First comes preparation of the body. This may involve washing, shaving, paring the nails, combing the hair, and dressing in burial garments.

The Torajan people of Indonesia have a two-stage process of preparation. In the earliest part of the ritual, the person is not considered dead, but "merely sick."[6] The body is treated with loving attention. It is "cleaned, wrapped in fine cloth, and arranged in a sitting position to be kept in the house, where it is visited, as if alive."[7] Just before the funeral, the body is laid out in a coffin and made ready for burial.

The ancient Egyptians are legendary for their elaborate burial preparations. The bodies of rulers and other important people were carefully mummified. This process involved removing the internal organs, preserving the body with chemicals, and wrapping it in multiple layers of bandages. Mummies have been found remarkably preserved after hundreds of years in the tomb.

Burial garments have included everything from simple linen shrouds to lavish attire that reflected the person's status in life. Kings and queens were dressed in their royal regalia, military men in their uniforms, and ordinary people in the clothing they liked best in life.

In the United States, funeral directors can choose from a vast array of garments designed for dressing the dead. These include everything from one-size-fits-all dress oxfords for men to "hostess gowns and brunch coats"[8] for women.

## Paying Last Respects

After a death, most cultures call for a period of deep mourning. In many societies, professional mourners make sure the deceased is properly lamented. They shriek and wail, cry piteously, and generally express grief in a form that is acceptable to the particular culture.

Mourning rituals in the home include such things as stopping clocks, covering mirrors or turning them toward the walls, and emptying water vessels; "the pouring out of water symbolizes the extinction of life."[9] Observant Jews rend (tear) their garments as a sign of grief.

This last custom is based upon several biblical references. For example, II Samuel 1:11 says that David and his soldiers "tore their clothes in sorrow"[10] upon hearing of the death of King Saul.

Prefuneral rituals often include a wake, or death watch. This is an around-the-clock vigil to ensure that the body will never be left alone during the time before burial. Wakes range from the somber and reverent to the riotous. For example, Irish wakes are famous for being noisy, disorderly events that involve a great deal of drinking and eating. This is not regarded as disrespectful. It is a rousing tribute to the deceased and a reaffirmation of life for the living.

Another prefuneral custom is the visitation. Friends of the deceased stop by to pray over the casket, or simply to sit quietly as a final gesture of respect. In the Jewish religion, the visitation occurs for eight days after the funeral.

In many parts of the world, visitations and wakes are held in the home of the deceased. In the United States the focus of last rites is changing from the home to the funeral chapel. Professional funeral directors handle everything from taking charge of the body after death to cremating it or laying it in the ground.

## The Last Farewell

The most common methods of sending the body to its final rest are burial in the ground and cremation. Burial at sea is also used but is generally limited to naval personnel, merchant marines, or those who die during a long voyage.

Funerals are typically a three-stage process. There is a service at a house of worship or funeral home, a procession to the place of burial or cremation, and a brief service committing the body to the flames or the grave. Within this basic pattern there is a wealth of room for cultural differences.

For example, in India cremation is the preferred method of handling the body. The deceased is grandly dressed and placed atop a funeral pyre (heap of flammable material). Flowers surround the body. Amid great ceremony, the fire is lit. In former times, widows were supposed to fling themselves onto the pyre and be burned alongside their husbands. The practice, known as suttee (from the Sanskrit *sati*, meaning "faithful wife") was outlawed in 1829.

In cultures that practiced earth burial, a variety of "grave goods" were buried with the deceased. Weapons, tools, amulets, valuable jewelry, and food have been found in tombs all over the world. The tombs of prominent people were elaborately furnished with items the person would presumably need in the afterlife. In some cultures, this included burying sacrificial victims to serve the needs of the deceased. For example, the kings of ancient China were buried with dogs, horses, and as many as three hundred human attendants. In ancient Egypt, wives, concubines, and servants were sealed alive into the tomb of a pharaoh.

Americans have a custom that is rare in the rest of the world—the open-casket funeral. By the mid-1990s, 68 percent of United States funerals featured an open casket.[11] The deceased are embalmed, carefully made up, and laid out in an elegant casket. The goal of the funeral director is to make the person look as if he or she is not dead, but merely asleep.

After the service, mourners file past the casket while hymns or funeral dirges (somber melodies) play softly in the background. Some people avert their eyes. Some linger or want to touch. Some break into tears and remark on how peaceful and lifelike the body appears.

Foreigners are often shocked by this display. An Englishwoman living in the United States wrote to Jessica Mitford about the funeral of an elderly coworker:

> After the service I could not understand why
> everyone was walking towards the coffin . . . but
> thought I had better follow the crowd. It shook me
> rigid to get there and find the casket open and
> poor old Oscar lying there in his brown tweed suit,
> wearing a suntan makeup and just the wrong
> shade of lipstick. . . . Then and there I decided
> that I could never face another American funeral—
> even dead.[12]

In the last half of the twentieth century, memorial services gained popularity. They may be held in addition to, or instead of, conventional funerals. The biggest difference between the two is that a funeral is held in the presence of the body, while the memorial is not.

Changing attitudes toward death have begun to transform both funerals and memorial services. Psychologist Tom Bruce, who teaches a class in death and dying, commented on this trend, "[M]aybe there's a better way to grieve. Maybe we can develop alternative rituals that help people feel, rather than just cost quite a lot of money and leave you with no sense of any kind of healing."[13]

Both funerals and memorial services are often followed by a reception in a social hall or the home of a family member. There is food and drink, friendly conversation, and sometimes mementos of the deceased such as photos, trophies, and awards.

## You Are Not Supposed to Cry

In most cultures, funerals are solemn occasions. While a certain cheerfulness may be appropriate at a reception, it is out of place at the funeral itself. There are, of course, exceptions to this general rule.

Torajan funerals are celebrations. Grieving is done during the elaborate ceremonies before the burial. The funeral itself is marked by feasting, dancing, colorful processions, boxing matches, and a good deal of neighborly gossip.[14]

The Nyakyusa people of Malawi (in southeast Africa) believe that laughter and good spirits at a funeral are a way of comforting the relatives of the deceased. "If we . . . sat sad and glum, then the grief of the relatives would far exceed ours. . . . And so we sit and talk and laugh and dance until the relatives laugh, too."[15]

Probably the most famous of all funeral celebrations is the New Orleans jazz funeral. Its foundation came from Africa, with people who were kidnapped from their homes and brought to the Americas as slaves. Many African cultures had a tradition of treating funerals as celebrations. In New Orleans, they began adding music to their funeral processions. Over time, the pattern for the jazz funeral developed.

"You're not supposed to cry at a funeral," a New Orleans performer told television journalist Charles Kuralt. "You're supposed to rejoice that another poor soul has escaped this vale of tears; at the very least you can be glad it wasn't you."[16]

In a traditional jazz funeral, the band leads the procession from the church or funeral parlor to the cemetery. The mood is somber, and so is the music. The band plays plaintive hymns and spirituals such as "Just a Closer Walk with Thee," or "Nearer My God to Thee."

After the graveside service, the band marches silently from the cemetery. The mourners follow. At a respectful distance, the lead trumpeter raises his horn and sounds a riff. The drummers pick up the beat. The rest of the instruments follow, launching into an exuberant tune, such as "When the Saints Go Marching In."

Brightly decorated umbrellas pop open like so many blossoming wildflowers as the mourners cast sadness aside, strutting and dancing to the relentless beat of the music. It is a reminder, says jazz musician Ellis Marsalis, "that there is something not only to mourn, but also to celebrate, even in death."[17]

## Tributes and Memorials

Over the course of human history, societies have developed many ways to honor and memorialize the deceased. Tombstones mark gravesites. Funerary urns hold the ashes of cremated bodies. These urns may be kept in the home, or placed in a mausoleum, which is a large building with crypts for bodies and/or niches for crematory urns.

Another alternative is the scattering of ashes, often at sea, or over some favorite landscape of the deceased. In British funerals, scattering is often done with a touch of whimsy. People go to great lengths to think up novel ways to dispose of their last remains. Methods have included everything from using the ashes as fertilizer on a beloved garden to sending them aloft in fireworks. One pub owner wanted his ashes used in an egg timer "so that he [could] carry on working."[18]

Tombstone design has also inspired much creativity. Grave markers used to be elaborate affairs, with beautiful carvings and epitaphs (inscriptions). Today, many cemeteries standardize their grounds by allowing only small brass plaques to adorn the graves. Though such cemeteries are undoubtedly tidier than older ones, they lose something in their careful uniformity.

People once gave a great deal of thought to the design of tombstones and the wording of inscriptions.

*Eighteenth-century tombstones in Durham, Connecticut. The winged faces on top represent guardian angels.*

Those with a creative bent would write their own epitaphs, often with ironic humor. British dramatist George Bernard Shaw wrote, "I knew if I hung around long enough this would happen."[19]

Poet John Gay (1688–1732) summed up his life and death in an epitaph of two lines:

*Life is a jest and all things show it.*
*I thought so once, but now I know it.*[20]

Comedian W. C. Fields, who was known for his droll humor, penned an unforgettable epitaph for himself: "On the Whole, I'd Rather Be in Philadelphia." Unfortunately, the Forest Lawn Cemetery in Glendale required standardized plaques. Fields's memorial gives only his name and dates of birth and death.[21]

Observances for the dead do not stop with burial or cremation. Most cultures have rituals to mark anniversaries of a particular death, as well as holidays commemorating the dead in general. Halloween was once a feast for the dead. The beginnings of trick-or-treat had nothing to do with kids, costumes, and candy. Poor people went door-to-door, promising to pray for the household's dead in return for soul cakes. Women baked dozens of these cakes for the occasion.

Jews observe the Yahrzeit (anniversary) of a death by going to the synagogue to recite the Kaddish (mourner's prayer) on each Yahrzeit of a parent's death. Some people also recite the prayer for other close relatives who have died. Yiskor, a memorial service for the dead, is an important part of observances on the Day of Atonement.

*Cemeteries have been regarded as fearsome places, where all manner of supernatural things can happen. Here, a man runs from a suddenly resurrected corpse.*

In Mexico and other Latin countries, the Day of the Dead is an important holiday—part tribute to the dead, part festival for the living. People decorate the graves of their dead and create memorial altars in their honor. These ofrendas (offerings) are personalized with memorabilia of the deceased, such as photos and a selection of his or her favorite possessions. They usually include flowers, candles, bright paper decorations, and fanciful reminders of death itself. Skulls made from spun sugar are a favorite, along with miniature tombstones and coffins.[22]

Imagination is the key to creating an effective altar. One fourth-grade class in California honored their deceased grandparents with a group altar. It included the children's drawings of skeletons playing basketball, fishing, and doing other things their grandparents had enjoyed in life.

## The Process of Grieving

When the funeral is over and outward life returns to normal, grieving relatives and friends face a difficult task. They have to work through their pain and learn how to live without the person who has died.

According to most grief counselors, the first year after a death is the hardest. Grief is fresh and painful. Daily life is filled with reminders of the one who has died. In a newsletter from the Hospice Foundation of America, Doctor of Divinity Paul E. Irion explains the importance of the first year:

> Why a year? Largely, it is to give you a chance to experience all of your . . . special days in new

ways without an important presence. You have, or will, come to the day which you always celebrated as your loved one's birthday. . . . Holidays like Thanksgiving, Christmas, or Chanukah are sharp reminders of your loss because they are when families gather. Inevitably you confront the first anniversary of the death of your loved one, and it all comes back to you.[23]

Grief does not magically disappear after that first anniversary. Dr. Kenneth J. Doka explains, "Most people take longer than a year to resolve grief. The issue after the first year is not *if* we're feeling better, but if we're feeling better *more* of the time. There will be ups and downs, but perhaps the down periods will be less intense and less frequent."[24]

According to *The Natural Death Handbook* of Britain's National Death Centre, grief is a process that passes through several stages: stunned disbelief, fierce pain, guilt, depression, and in time, acceptance of the loss.[25]

Teenagers pass through these stages differently from adults. They are already in a time of transition. Their lives and bodies are changing, and each change brings a loss. With each step toward adulthood, the teenager is losing a piece of his or her childhood.

When the death of a parent, sibling, or other important person is added to these normal changes, the sense of loss can be overwhelming. One notable difference between teens and adults is the way they react immediately after the death.

Bereavement counselor Linda Cunningham explains,

> Many teens experience what I call "automatic
> pilot": they function as usual but with a feeling
> that "this really didn't happen." Teenagers . . .
> may show little signs of grieving in the
> beginning. This numbness . . . is an important
> [way of] coping . . . and should be respected.[26]

When the numbness wears off and the grief and
guilt set in, teenagers may face what Cunningham
calls "unusual happenings."[27]

"It is not . . . uncommon for a bereaved teenager
to hear the voice of the deceased or feel as though
they see that person passing by or in a crowd,"
Cunningham says.[28] Thoughts of suicide may occur,
and many grieving teens are vulnerable to alcohol or
drug abuse.

Teenage anger can be intense. Especially when
the person who died is a parent, the teenager may
feel abandoned. He or she becomes angry at the parent for dying and often experiences crushing guilt
over these feelings. It is important for a grieving teen
to know that this anger is entirely normal. It does not
mean that he or she is a bad person or did not love
the deceased parent.

Counselors or others who deal with grieving
teenagers try to help them express their anger in non-
harmful ways. These methods might include
screaming, crying, hitting a punching bag, or pound-
ing a mattress.

Teenagers can work through grief by talking out
their feelings with a counselor or trusted friend.
Keeping a journal of dreams and stray ideas can help
give focus to the grieving process. In bereavement

groups, counselors sometimes use role-playing. Someone plays the part of the person who has died. The participant tells that person the things he or she never got the chance to say to the deceased loved one.

Coming to terms with grief is a long, slow process. It involves learning to live without the person who has died and learning to accept the loss and treasure the memories. It also involves coming to terms with death itself. Grieving helps to make us aware that death is part of life and that we, too, will someday die.

# 5

# Visions of the Afterworld

On the long, evolutionary road to humankind, death awareness developed slowly. Anthropologists (scientists who study the origin and development of humankind) know this by the manner of burials. The earliest ancestors of humanity disposed of their dead as they might the carcass of a dead animal. The body was not adorned, wrapped, or placed in a symbolic position. There were no worldly goods buried with the body or markers to show where the body lay.

According to anthropologist Richard Leakey, ritual burials indicate the beginning of death awareness. "The earliest

72

evidence of deliberate burial . . . occurs very late in [human] history. It comes with the Neanderthals . . . not much more than 100,000 years ago."[1]

After early humans figured out that death was forever, they began to grieve for lost companions. With grief came rites and rituals to honor the deceased. The last stage in the process of death awareness was the realization that everyone will someday die. Nobody knows exactly when people acquired this knowledge.

Whenever it happened, we can be sure of one thing: Death awareness made people wonder about the meaning of life. Richard Leakey explains:

> Once consciousness passed the threshold of self-awareness and death awareness, there welled up in the human mind the Big Question: Why? It is not a straight request for an answer; it is a search for meaning in the midst of uncertainty. What is the meaning of my life? What is the meaning of the world I find myself in? How did the Universe come to be?[2]

People looked outside themselves for answers to these questions. Their search was the beginning of myth, religion, and philosophy.

## "The Death Thing"

"The football I can take care of. It's the death thing that I can't control,"[3] said Al Davis, owner of the Oakland Raiders football team. Davis is known for being preoccupied with death and with the loss of control it represents. At the very least, death is an unknown. For most people that is reason enough to dread and fear it.

Many people believe that the soul survives physical death. In some traditions the soul lives eternally in a world beyond this one. In others, it is reborn to live other lives. Nonreligious people often accept death as an end. They try to find meaning without reference to an afterlife.

Not all of them succeed. For example, one patient confided to Dr. Groopman that he feared dying because "after death . . . it's just nothingness."[4] Dr. Groopman asked why that was scary. "[It] would be the same as before we were born. Is that terrifying, to be unborn?"[5]

To many people, the idea of being "unborn" is terrifying indeed. It means extinction, the end of the self. That frightening prospect strips life of all meaning.

To some, *all* human existence is pointless. It is "a tale told by an idiot, full of sound and fury, signifying nothing," were the words of William Shakespeare.[6]

British philosopher Alfred North Whitehead saw life as a process. In this process, "all elements in the universe—from the light waves of a distant star to a human being living in Boise, Idaho—are interrelated."[7] This means that everything that exists has an effect on the whole.

Some effects are small and some are large. Obviously, a supernova changes the universe more than one human being. A human being changes it more than an amoeba. Still, in the view of Whitehead's philosophy, no life is insignificant. We can all say truthfully that the universe would not have been the same without us.

Some believe that the meaning of their lives rests in the memory of others. The Jewish tradition, for example, emphasizes memory as a form of immortality. A meditation before the Kaddish (mourner's prayer), makes this clear:

> At this sacred moment, we turn our thoughts to those we love who have gone from life. We recall the joy of their companionship. We feel a pang, the echo of that . . . grief when first [they died]. Now we know that they will never vanish, so long as

*The ancient Greeks believed that Charon transported the newly departed to the underworld by ferry. People were buried with a coin in their mouth to pay Charon for his services.*

heart and thought remain within us. By love are they remembered, and in memory they live.[8]

Some people find comfort in the idea of living on in memory, or in connectedness to the process of life. Others will settle for nothing less than survival of the self. As Dr. Groopman's patient put it, "I don't ask for heaven. I'd take hell. Just to *be*."[9]

## The Heavenly Home

Both Christians and Muslims believe there is an afterworld where the self survives intact. Both have a heaven and a hell. In the sixteenth century, the Catholic Church added purgatory. This was a "fire in which the souls of the pious are purified by a temporary punishment so that [they may enter] . . . the eternal country."[10]

Christianity and Islam descended from Judaism. From Judaism, they inherited an ethical code and a belief in one God. Their ideas about the afterlife are their own. Ancient Judaism was very much of this world, rather than the next. "[T]here was no heaven or hell, no state of conscious existence similar to the one we enjoy in this life," says Dr. Groopman.[11]

The Book of Daniel, which was written around 165 B.C., contains the first clear reference to resurrection in Jewish scripture. It states that at the end of time "many of those who lie dead in the ground will rise from death. Some of them will be given eternal life, and others will receive nothing but eternal shame and disgrace. Everyone who has been wise will shine as bright as the sky above, and everyone who has led others to please God will shine like the stars."[12]

The dwelling place of the righteous was not heaven, but a transformed and perfected earth. This earthly paradise theme also occurred in Greek, Roman, and Celtic cultures.

From the time of Homer (ninth century B.C.), Greek poets described "a land of music, dancing, sunny meadows, flowers, fountains, and sweet refreshment."[13] In this land, "death and disease have no dominion and no one lacks for anything."[14] The Roman Elysian Fields and the Celtic Blessed Isles are described in similar terms.

In Christian belief, the immortal self is not only a spirit. In some sense, it is a body as well. St. Paul explained in a passage about the resurrection of the dead:

> It will happen suddenly, quicker than the blink of an eye. At the sound of the last trumpet the dead will be raised. We will all be changed, so that we will never die again. Our dead and decaying bodies will be changed into bodies that won't die or decay. The bodies we now have are weak and can die. But they will be changed into bodies that are eternal.[15]

According to religious studies professor Jeffrey Burton Russell, this resurrected body was a physical one "that eats, excretes, breathes, circulates the blood, and fires neurons."[16] Today, many Christians emphasize spiritual rather than physical resurrection. One thing remains constant: The self survives. People in the Christian heaven retain their memories and personalities. They are in some way recognizable to each other.

## Hellfire and Damnation

This self-awareness also exists in hell. If it did not, then the torments of hell would not actually hurt. The eternal punishment of sinners would not be "real." In Christianity and Islam, the torments are not only real, but eternal.

The Koran (Muslim scripture) says that "whoso rebels against God and His Apostle [Mohammed], verily, for him is the fire of hell . . . to dwell therein for ever and for [always]."[17] The sufferings of hell are described in the punishments of "those who misbelieve."[18]

> [For] them are cut out garments of fire, there shall be poured over their heads boiling water, wherewith what is in their bellies shall be dissolved and their skins, too. . . . Whenever they desire to come forth therefrom through pain, they are sent back into it: And taste ye the torment of the burning.[19]

The Christian hell is every bit as distasteful. The biblical book of Revelation says that sinners "shall be tormented with fire and brimstone. . . . And the smoke of their torment ascendeth up for ever and ever; and they shall have no rest day nor night, who worship the beast and his image."[20]

Later Christian writers used their own images of hell to scare sinners into repentance. In the eighteenth century, for example, Alphonso de' Liguori founded an order (religious group) "to send hellfire preachers to Catholic pulpits."[21] His descriptions were both graphic and terrifying:

> The unhappy wretch will be surrounded by fire like wood in a furnace. He will find an abyss of fire below, an abyss above, and an abyss on every side. If he touches, if he sees, if he breathes, he touches, sees, breathes only fire. He will be in fire like a fish in water. This fire will not only surround the damned, but it will enter into his bowels to torment him. His body will become all fire, so that the bowels within him will burn, his heart will

*Monstrous images of torment and suffering appear in descriptions of hell. Here, the devil roasts the Emperor Napoleon over an everlasting fire.*

burn in his bosom, his brains in his head, his blood in his veins, even the marrow in his bones; each [sinner] will in himself become a furnace of fire. [22]

## The Wheel of Death and Rebirth

Personal immortality in an eternal afterworld is a Western religious idea. Eastern religions have a different view. Traditions such as Hinduism and Buddhism accept reincarnation, in which the soul is reborn again and again. The soul lives many lifetimes before it is finally absorbed into the infinite. The personality, which is what most of us mean when we speak of the self, does not survive physical death.

There is hell aplenty in Eastern religion. "Hindus number up to several million of them, while Buddhists count from eight hells to several thousand."[23] Though these hells are suitably horrendous, they are not permanent. In this sense, they have more in common with purgatory than with the Christian hell.

Souls suffer according to their sins in life. Then they are reborn to learn the lessons of another existence. The doctrine of karma determines the circumstances of each new life. For example, a man who mistreats women might be reborn as a woman who is victimized by men.

Karma continues through countless lifetimes, until the soul has worked out its own salvation. When the soul is freed from the cycle of rebirth, it leaves personal identity behind to merge into the infinite.

*French psychic Camille Flammarion attempted to prove that the soul survives after death.*

Eastern and Western religions not only have different views about the afterlife, but about reality itself. Judaism, Christianity, and Islam are *monotheistic* (one god) faiths. Hinduism and Buddhism are *monistic* (one reality). Everything from gods and galaxies to bacteria and subatomic particles are part of this single reality. So are we. The self that many value so highly is, by nature, temporary. Letting it go is the last step into an unchanging, eternal reality.

## Visits and Visions

There are people who believe they have seen the afterworld through visions or near death experiences (NDEs). In almost all cases, these people return to normal life with a changed perspective. Death no longer holds terrors for them. They feel absolutely certain that there is, indeed, a life after this one.

The earliest English account of an NDE comes from the Venerable Bede in the eighth century. Bede tells the story of a "man who was thought to be dead."

> I was guided by a handsome man in a shining robe.
> . . . When we reached the top of a wall, there was
> . . . a wide and pleasant meadow, with light . . .
> that seemed brighter than daylight or the midday
> sun. I was very reluctant to leave, for I was
> enraptured [delighted] by the place's pleasantness
> and beauty and by the company I saw there.[24]

In 1992, Bette J. Eadie sparked renewed interest in NDEs with her book *Embraced by the Light*. In 1973, Eadie "died" after surgery. Her breathing and heartbeat stopped. Her body shut down. There was no evidence of brain activity. Determined efforts by doctors and hospital personnel revived her.

During the time that she was clinically dead, Eadie had an experience that changed her forever. Twenty years later she described it in detail. Other NDEs echo her themes of light, pleasant vistas, glowing guides, peace, and joy.

Yvonne Malik remembered being "surrounded by light, it was golden yellow, very bright and seemed to become brighter and whiter. There was no need to squint as it was not painful. . . . The light itself had a personality, it *was* joy. The air itself seemed to be full of love and joy."[25]

One of the most stunning accounts of the afterworld is neither a mystic vision nor an NDE. It is a work of literature, *The Divine Comedy* by Dante Alighieri (1265–1321). *The Divine Comedy* occupies a special place in Christian (particularly Catholic) beliefs about heaven, hell, and purgatory. While not regarded as scripture, it is considered by many to be "inspired by God."[26]

*The Divine Comedy* consists of three books: *The Inferno* (hell), *The Purgatorio* (purgatory), and *The Paradiso* (paradise, or heaven). The work is cast as a pilgrimage, or journey, through the three realms. Dante sets the scene in the famous passage that begins *The Inferno*:

> Midway upon the journey of our life
> I found myself within a forest dark,
> For the straightforward pathway had been lost.
> Ah me! how hard a thing it is to say
> What was this forest savage, rough, and stern,

Throughout history, the quest for physical immortality has been associated with evil. Here, a witch brews a potion with the aid of a demon. Death lurks in the background.

Which in the very thought renews the fear.
So bitter is it, death is little more;
But of the good to treat, which there I found,
Speak will I of the other things I saw there.[27]

Dante's hell has nine levels, or circles, each more terrible than the last. His purgatory is a mountain "in the midst of the southern sea,"[28] where souls dwell according to the seven cardinal sins (pride, envy, anger, sloth, greed, gluttony, lust). Paradise, or heaven, ascends through nine levels to a tenth heaven. In this place of light "there is no dimension, no time, no space."[29]

Descriptions of the afterworld are shaped by culture. Psychologists Karlis Osis and Erlendur Haaraldsson demonstrated this in a study comparing the deathbed visions of Christians and Hindus. They found that "Christians tended to [see] angels, Jesus, or the Virgin Mary, whereas Hindus would usually see Yama (the god of death), one of his messengers. . . . or some other deity."[30]

Visions and NDEs can be studied and compared, but they cannot be proved or disproved. Even the most brilliant of scientists cannot put eternity into a test tube. We may accept or reject scriptures, literature, and personal testimonies, but we simply cannot know the afterworld in the way we can know the location of Kansas or that two plus two equals four. When all is said and done, belief—or nonbelief—in an afterlife is a matter of faith, or its lack.

# 6

# How Long Is Long Enough?

**"I** don't want to achieve immortality through my work," said filmmaker Woody Allen, "I want to achieve it through not dying."[1] Allen's humor points to an important idea. Some people are not content to hope for an afterlife, nor can they accept their own extinction. They fight death every step of the way, and would defy it altogether if they could.

How long is long enough? The answer to that question is not the same for everybody; it never has been. Threescore and ten (70) years, said the Bible, but science has stretched that limit. Today, we have therapies to cure disease, repair injury, and extend the human life span.

## Making Tradeoffs

In spite of their fear of death, many people take up dangerous activities or occupations. Willingness to risk life and limb is part of the job description for firefighters, police officers, and soldiers. It is part of the thrill for those who take up sports such as sky-diving, or bungee jumping.

Not everyone who risks his or her life does it in such a dramatic fashion. Some do it through a series of small, quiet choices. They simply refuse to make longevity the be-all and end-all of their existence.

For example, the people of New Orleans are famous for cheerfully ignoring all the medical research about diet and longevity. Obviously, not everyone in New Orleans does this, but studies show that 38 percent of the city's population is obese.[2] That is the highest rate in the nation. The average life span in New Orleans is sixty-four years, compared with a national average of seventy-three years.[3]

It is not that people do not realize what they are doing, according to city coroner Frank Minyard. He sums up the attitude in a single sentence: "It's not the quantity of life that counts in New Orleans, it's the quality."[4] Minyard is not just speaking as a coroner. His hobby is playing trumpet in jazz funerals.

Quality of life means different things to different people. For some, it means pursuing a dream regardless of the cost. Carrie Reed of Sacramento,

California, is a case in point. After a lifetime of wanting a child, she became pregnant at the age of forty. In the fourth month of her pregnancy, the doctors wanted to test her for leukemia.

Reed faced a cruel choice. If she had leukemia, immediate chemotherapy could save her life, but it would kill the unborn child. If she waited until after the birth, it might be too late.

In spite of the risk, and against her doctor's advice, Reed chose motherhood. She refused to be tested for leukemia until after the baby was born. She delivered a healthy son in July 1998. Two and a half months later, Carrie Reed died of leukemia.

"Being a mother was all [Carrie] ever wanted in life," said Reed's sister Karen Jordan. "At least she got to experience it for a little while. She had her dream."[5]

For every Carrie Reed who would sacrifice time for a dream, there are probably a few dozen who would choose survival. A university study of 414 people between the ages of 80 and 98 turned up some surprising results. All these subjects were hospitalized with serious illnesses. Some were in considerable pain.

Researchers asked how much time they would trade for a shorter life in excellent health. More than 40 percent said they would not bargain away any time. They wanted to live as long as possible, whatever their state of health. About 28 percent were willing to give up one month out of twelve. Only 6 percent said they would give away a year of life in their present condition for two weeks of good health.

**SWELL STRUGGLING WITH THE CIG'RETTE POISONER.**

*People risk shortening their lives in many ways. In this 1882 engraving, cigarettes form the skeleton of a deadly serpent.*

"That means patients were pretty satisfied with their life as it was," said lead researcher Dr. Joel Tsevat. "Even though they weren't very healthy, they just wanted to hang in there."[6]

## Cheating Death

Since humans first confronted the fact of death, there have been those who dreamed of cheating the Grim Reaper of his prize. In reality, this has never happened. In literature and myth, it happens all the time, often with disastrous results.

A misspoken word or a fatal omission can lead to tragedy. The Greek tale of Eos and Tithonos is a good example. Eos, goddess of dawn, fell in love with a handsome youth named Tithonos. She begged Zeus, king of the gods, to give Tithonos eternal life. After Zeus granted her wish, Eos realized she had made a terrible mistake. She had forgotten to ask for eternal youth for Tithonos.

The goddess of dawn watched helplessly as Tithonos became a shrunken, shriveled horror, whom she shut away in a closet. Only his voice remained, clear and strong as ever, speaking from the darkness of his prison.

A similar theme appears in the film *Death Becomes Her*. Two women who cheerfully loathe each other take a mysterious potion. It is supposed to keep them young and beautiful. Too late, they learn that immortality comes at a price. Because their bodies do not change, they cannot heal. Every injury, every scar, lasts forever.

*The legendary Doctor Faustus, written of in plays and novels, sold his soul to the devil for an extra twenty-four years of life. During that time, every form of pleasure and knowledge would be his. Here, the devil comes to collect his due.*

The two characters are doomed to spend eternity endlessly patching each other back together. The film ends with them falling down a flight of stairs and literally shattering into pieces. Even the pieces are still alive, talking and arguing as the screen fades to black.

In the children's book *Tuck Everlasting*, author Natalie Babbitt tells the story of a family that discovers the fountain of youth in a forest. When a young girl named Winnie learns their secret, the father of this immortal family tells her the price of eternal life:

> It's a wheel, Winnie. Everything's a wheel, turning and turning, never stopping. The frogs is part of it, and the bugs, and the fish, and the wood thrush, too. And people. But never the same ones. Always coming in new, always growing and changing, and always moving on. That's the way it's supposed to

be. That's the way it is. Being part of the whole thing, that's the blessing. But it's passing us by, us Tucks. Living's heavy work, but off to one side, the way *we* are, it's useless, too. It don't make sense. If I knowed how to climb back on the wheel, I'd do it in a minute. You can't have living without dying. So you can't call it living, what we got. We just *are*, we just *be*, like rocks beside the road.[7]

In real life, many have searched for what the fictional Tucks found. The Spanish explorer Juan Ponce de León (c. 1460–1521) sailed to the New World in search of the fountain. He believed it was on one of the tropical islands that dot the Caribbean. What he found was the peninsula that became the state of Florida. Ponce de León died in 1521, possibly still believing that somewhere there was a magical island, where living waters flowed from a hidden spring.

## Freezing Time

In 1962, Robert C. W. Ettinger wrote *The Prospect of Immortality* and launched the cryonics movement. His idea was to freeze clinically dead people in liquid nitrogen. This would put them in stasis (a state of absolute and unchanging stillness) until "future technology [could] deal with their problems."[8]

An organization known as the Cryonics Institute offers this technology to those who want it. In the mid-1990s, the Institute's fee for preparing, freezing, and maintaining cryonic storage was twenty-eight thousand dollars.[9]

Even supporters of cryonics admit that the

techniques are not yet perfected. There has been some success with freezing and reviving insects and mollusks. Human embryos are frozen for later use. When defrosted and implanted in a uterus, they have produced normal pregnancies.

There is a huge difference between preserving an embryo and preserving an entire human body. Nobody knows if people in cryonic stasis can ever be revived. In spite of this, some people are willing to take the chance. To them, even a slim possibility of immortality is worth twenty-eight thousand dollars.

## The Immortalists

The late twentieth century produced a new chapter in the story of humankind's long struggle with death: immortalism. Modern immortalists place their faith in scientific advances that might one day bring "indefinitely extended life."[10]

Developing new and better ways to cure illness and repair injury is part of this process. So are methods for preventing damage in the first place. Scientists are investigating deadly and incurable diseases such as Alzheimer's, ALS, and Parkinson's.

This research has already produced exciting results. For example, scientists identified the genetic defect that causes cystic fibrosis (CF) in 1989. Just one year later, the National Institutes of Health introduced a healthy gene into cystic fibrosis cells. The altered cells began to function normally.

CF is an inherited disease that "causes the mucus-secreting glands to go into overdrive."[11] This clogs the lungs and bronchial tubes with phlegm. It also affects the pancreas. Children born with CF rarely live past their twenties.

Success in a laboratory is a far cry from success with living people. Still, gene replacement offers exciting possibilities. It could one day cure CF and other inherited disorders, such as sickle cell anemia and certain forms of cancer and heart disease.

Research into brain chemistry could yield a cure for Alzheimer's and other diseases of the nervous system. Research into cell regeneration could solve the problem of transplant rejection. The body's immune system would not attack a replacement organ grown from its own cells. Antirejection drugs would no longer be necessary. The whole uncomfortable process of "harvesting" organs from the dead would become a thing of the past.

## Dr. Hayflick and Mrs. Lacks

Replacing organs, eliminating inherited defects, and curing disease would allow more people to live longer, pain-free lives. It would not allow them to live forever. Medical miracles notwithstanding, time catches up with everyone.

To increase our life span to anything approaching immortality, we would have to cure the one "disease" that afflicts us all: old age. Some people say this cannot be done. Our bodies are "programmed" to slow down and eventually stop functioning.

In the 1970s, biologist Leonard Hayflick began to study cell reproduction. He worked with fibroblast

*Death, the inescapable hunter, comes out of a dark cave to claim new victims.*

cells. These are the cells that form scar tissue around a wound and connective tissue throughout the body. When he grew fibroblasts in the laboratory, they "quickly began dividing [reproducing]. But soon their rate of division slowed down. After a few weeks, they stopped altogether and eventually died."[12]

They reproduced about fifty times, and then died. This limit applied even when cell reproduction was artificially interrupted. Fibroblasts that had divided twenty times were frozen in liquid nitrogen. When they were defrosted, they made thirty more divisions before dying.

The number of times a cell will reproduce has become known as the Hayflick limit. Different types of cells have different Hayflick limits. As they reach those limits and begin to die, the body ages. The challenge for science is to find a way to reset the clock.

Enter Henrietta Lacks, a cancer patient who died in 1951. Researchers kept some of her cancer cells to study. Nearly half a century later, those cells are still alive and still reproducing themselves. As far as anyone can tell, they are immortal.

> They have escaped whatever internal clock there is in normal cells that sets the Hayflick limit. . . . They do not [grow old] and die of internal causes, although they can certainly be killed. Unless they are stopped by outside agents, tumor cells continue growing, which is what makes them deadly when they grow inside a human body.[13]

The obvious question is why? What allows cancer cells to escape the Hayflick limit while normal cells do not? The answer may be in a part of the human cell known as a telomere, which protects the cell from damage during reproduction. Each time a cell divides, its telomere gets shorter. When enough of the telomere is gone, the cell dies.

In 1997, researchers found that the telomeres of cancer cells do not shorten as the cell divides. The reason seems to be an enzyme called telomerase. Cancer cells produce it in quantity and normal cells do not. By adding telomerase to laboratory cultures of normal human cells, researchers succeeded in rebuilding the telomeres.

According to Dr. Ben Bova, president emeritus of the National Space Society, these rebuilt cells "reproduced well past their Hayflick limits, giving powerful evidence that telomeres have a decisive influence on cellular [aging] and may indeed be 'the clock of aging.'"[14] Although "powerful evidence" is not the same as proven fact, the telomerase research is widely regarded as promising.

Antiaging research still has a long way to go. No one can say with certainty what the outcome will be. Even if scientists find the mechanism responsible for aging and disable it, death will continue to be a fact of life. People will still have auto accidents. They will still get killed in wars and violent assaults. Thousands will die each year in natural disasters such as hurricanes and earthquakes.

Everything dies sooner or later, even stars and planets. According to cosmologists, the universe itself will one day cease to exist. Death is so woven into the fabric of life that it is impossible to imagine existence without it; yet it is equally impossible to imagine our own extinction.

This fundamental conflict underlies human attitudes toward death, life, and meaning. Science may extend our lives and cure our ills, but it cannot answer our ultimate questions about why we are alive in the first place and what will happen to us after we die. Religion gives answers for people of faith, but not everybody can accept those answers.

Despite all that humankind has learned and

thought and believed, death still remains the ultimate mystery. Whatever advances may come now that we have entered the new millennium, how we deal with that mystery will continue to define our attitudes toward life as well as toward death. Only time will tell if our attitudes and beliefs will change.

# Glossary

**advance directive**—Instructions left by a person detailing his or her desires in the event of serious disability or terminal illness.

**AIDS**—A disease of the immune system.

**AIDS cocktail**—A mixture of drugs for treating the disease.

**Alzheimer's disease**—A degenerative disease of the brain characterized by loss of memory, judgment, and self-identity.

**amyotrophic lateral sclerosis (ALS)**—A degenerative disease of the nervous system characterized by gradual loss of physical function.

**angina pectoris**—Spasms of the heart muscle.

**artery**—Part of the circulatory system; a vessel that carries blood away from the heart.

**automatic functions**—Self-regulating functions, such as breathing and heartbeat.

**brain death**—Cessation of all function in the brain.

**brain stem**—The part of the brain that controls automatic functions such as breathing and heartbeat.

**Brompton cocktail**—A mixture of painkilling drugs given to terminally ill patients.

**cancer**—A tumor that grows uncontrollably, destroying healthy cells.

**catheter**—A flexible tube inserted into the body to withdraw fluids.

**cholera**—An infectious epidemic disease characterized by severe diarrhea, dehydration, vomiting, and muscle cramps.

**chronic**—Lasting for a long time.

**clinical death**—The end of all bodily functions.

**coma**—Profound unconsciousness.

**cystic fibrosis**—Inherited disease that causes the mucus-secreting glands to overproduce, clogging the lungs with thick mucus.

**death agonies**—Jerky, reflexive movements at the time of death.

**degenerative**—Gradually worsening.

**dehydration**—Loss of water in bodily tissues.

**dementia**—Loss or impairment of mental function.

**Down syndrome**—A form of mental retardation.

**early death**—Death within hours after an injury.

**Ebola**—A virus that causes a particularly deadly form of hemorrhagic fever.

**epidemic**—Any rapidly spreading infectious disease that attacks many people at the same time.

**euthanasia**—Literally, "good death" (Greek); causing painless death to end a patient's suffering.

**Hayflick limit**—The number of times a cell will reproduce before dying.

**HIV**—The virus that causes AIDS.

**hemorrhagic fever**—A disease characterized by fever and heavy bleeding.

**hospice**—A program or institution that specializes in comfort care of the terminally ill.

**immediate death**—Death within minutes of an injury.

**immune system**—The bodily system that secretes infection-fighting substances.

**intravenous**—Within a vein.

**jaundice**—A diseased condition of the liver that produces marked yellowing of the skin.

**late death**—Death days or weeks after an injury.

**Marburg virus**—A disease agent that causes a type of hemorrhagic fever.

**palliative care**—Care directed at comfort rather than cure.

**Parkinson's disease**—A degenerative disease of the nervous system characterized by tremors and loss of coordination.

**persistent vegetative state**—Deep and irreversible coma marked by the loss of higher brain functions.

**quadriplegia**—Paralysis from the neck down in all four limbs.

**slippery slope**—The idea that an act that is not immoral in itself can lead in time to acts that are immoral and/or illegal.

**smallpox**—A contagious disease marked by fever and skin eruptions.

**sudden death**—Uunexpected death from illness, occurring within a few hours after the beginning of symptoms.

**suicide**—The taking of one's own life.

**terminal illness**—Term applied when a patient is expected to die within six months.

**ventilator**—An artificial breathing machine.

**yellow fever**—An infectious intestinal disease transmitted by mosquitoes. Symptoms include jaundice, vomiting, and degeneration of the liver.

**whole brain death**—When all brain activity ceases, the patient may be considered dead.

# Chapter Notes

## Chapter 1. The Way We Die

1. "Brain-dead Florida Girl Will Be Sent Home on Life Support," *The New York Times*, February 19, 1994, p. 9.

2. Sherwin B. Nuland, M.D., *How We Die: Reflections on Life's Final Chapter* (New York: Alfred A. Knopf, 1994), p. 1.

3. Ibid., p. 18.

4. Ibid.

5. Frank Ryan, M.D., *Virus X: Tracking the New Killer Plagues—Out of the Present and Into the Future* (Boston: Little, Brown and Co., 1997), p. 8.

6. Ibid., p. 167.

7. Ben Bova, M.D., *Immortality: How Science Is Extending Your Life Span—And Changing the World* (New York: Avon Books, 1998), p. 7.

8. Diane Sugg, "Debating Ethics of Medicine: Little Consensus Seen at Capital Symposium," *Sacramento Bee*, June 27, 1998, p. B1.

9. Nuland, p. 10.

10. Marilyn Webb, *The Good Death: The New American Search to Reshape the End of Life* (New York: Bantam Books, 1997), pp. 133–134.

11. Ibid., p. 140.

12. Ibid., p. 143.

## Chapter 2. Facing the End

1. Elisabeth Kübler-Ross, M.D., *On Death and Dying* (New York: Touchstone Books, 1997), p. 16.

2. Tom Philip, "Dignified Death Guidelines Urged," *Sacramento Bee*, November 12, 1996, p. B1.

3. Sherwin B. Nuland, M.D., *How We Die: Reflections on Life's Final Chapter* (New York: Alfred A. Knopf, 1994), p. 43.

4. Marilyn Webb, *The Good Death: The New American Search to Reshape the End of Life* (New York: Bantam Books, 1997), p. 397.

5. Ibid., p. 400.

6. Ibid.

7. S. Richardson, "Crushing HIV," *Discover*, January 1997, pp. 28–29.

8. Cynthia Hubert, "Transplant Pioneer Loses Battle for Life," *Sacramento Bee*, May 25, 1997, p. A1.

9. Kübler-Ross, pp. 94–95.

10. Ibid., p. 99.

11. Ibid.

12. Ibid., p. 124.

13. Susan L. Crowley and Leah K. Glasheen, "Choosing Hospice: Getting the Care You Need," *AARP Bulletin*, vol. 39, no. 6, June 1998, p. 14.

14. Judith C. Ahronheim, M.D., "Emerging End-of-Life Care: Understanding Palliative Care," *The Newsletter of Choice in Dying*, vol. 5, no. 4, Winter 1996, <http://www.choices.org/newsw96.htm> (May 22, 1999).

15. American Academy of Family Physicians, "Advance Directives and Do-Not-Resuscitate Orders: What You Need to Know," University of Iowa, 1994, <http://www.vh.org/Patients/IHB/FamilyPractice/AFP/November/NovTwo.html> (April 12, 1999).

16. "Shape Your Health Care Future with HEALTH CARE ADVANCE DIRECTIVES," American Association of Retired Persons, ABA Commission on Legal Problems of the Elderly, American Medical Association, 1995, <http://www.ama-assn.org/public/booklets/livgwill.htm> (April 12, 1999).

17. Ibid.

18. Ibid.

19. Ibid.

## Chapter 3. Choosing Death

1. Bonnie Johnson, Julie Greenwalt, and Susan Hauser, "Up Front: A Vital Woman Chooses Death, When Disease Threatened Her Dignity, Janet Adkins Sought a Doctor's Help to End Her Joyous Life," *People*, June 25, 1990, p. 40.

2. Marilyn Webb, *The Good Death: The New American Search to Reshape the End of Life* (New York: Bantam Books, 1997), p. 325.

3. William M. "Mike" Hurley, "Biblical Ethics and Euthanasia," 1998 <http://www.texramp.net/~whurley/euthanas.htm> (April 12, 1999).

4. Jerome Groopman, M.D., *The Measure of Our Days: New Beginnings at Life's End* (New York: Viking Books, 1997), p. 141.

5. Edgar Sanchez, "Sandra Jensen Back in Hospital. Condition Fair. Her Donor ID'D as Teen," *Sacramento Bee*, March 4, 1996, p. B1.

6. Sherwin B. Nuland, M.D., *How We Die: Reflections on Life's Final Chapter* (New York: Alfred A. Knopf, 1994), p. 156.

7. Derek Humphry, "Why I Believe in Voluntary Euthanasia: The Case for Rational Suicide," 1995 <http://www.rights.org/~deathnet/Humphry_essay.html> (April 12, 1999).

8. Layne Cameron, "Interview: Dr. Timothy Quill—Merciful Medicine," *The American Legion* magazine, October 1997, vol. 143, no. 4, n.p., <http://www.legion.org/pubs/1997/mercifull0.htm> (June 2, 1999).

9. Thomas Maier, "Suicide Law: Year 1/Few in Oregon Have Asked for Help in Dying," *Newsday*, November 3, 1998, p. C03.

10. Timothy Egan, "Voters Put Oregon on New Frontier Assisted-Suicide Law's Easy Win Shows Rapid Change in Public Views," *Rocky Mountain News*, November 8, 1997, p. 62A.

11. Kim Murphy, "Oregon Faces Wrenching Vote on Suicide Law," *The Los Angeles Times*, November 3, 1997, p. A1.

12. Charles Ornstein, "Woman Dies in First Publicized Case under Oregon Suicide Law," *The Dallas Morning News*, March 26, 1998, p. 3A.

13. Derek Humphry, *Final Exit: The Practicalities of Self-Deliverance and Assisted Suicide for the Dying* (New York: Dell Trade Paperback, 1996), p. 62.

14. Robert Jay Lifton, *The Nazi Doctors: Medical Killing and the Psychology of Genocide* (New York: Basic Books, Inc., 1986), p. 14.

15. Ibid., p. 142.

16. Todd Nissen, "U.S. Television to Show Kevorkian's Euthanasia Video," *Reuters Ltd.*, November 20, 1998.

17. Associated Press, "*60 Minutes* to Air Explicit Kevorkian Tape," November 20, 1998, p. A15.

18. "No Gray Area for Kevorkian Now: Videotaped Injection Death Challenges Law," *Sacramento Bee*, November 21, 1998, p. 1A.

19. Eric Slater, "Kevorkian Is Sentenced to 10 to 25 Years," *The Los Angeles Times*, April 14, 1999, p. 1A.

20. Lifton, p. 141.

## Chapter 4. Saying Goodbye

1. Laurence Bergreen, *Capone: The Man and the Era* (New York: Simon & Schuster, 1994), p. 136.

2. Elisabeth Kübler-Ross, M.D., *On Death and Dying* (New York: Touchstone Books, 1997), p. 19.

3. George Seldes, ed., *The Great Thoughts* (New York: Ballantine Books, 1996), p. 346.

4. Nigel Barley, *Grave Matters: A Lively History of Death Around the World* (New York: Henry Holt and Company, 1997), p. 32.

5. Ibid., p. 33.

6. Rita and Jim Ariyoshi, "As Fleeting as Mist: Funeral Celebrations in Torajaland," News World Communication, Inc., *The World & I*, vol. 10, February 1, 1995, p. 232.

7. Ibid.

8. Jessica Mitford, *The American Way of Death Revisited* (New York: Alfred A. Knopf, 1998), p. 34.

9. Rabbi Tzvi Rabinowicz, *A Guide to Life: Jewish Laws and Customs of Mourning* (Northvale, N.J.: Jason Aronson, Inc., 1989), p. 24.

10. II Samuel 1:11, *Holy Bible*, Contemporary English Version (New York: American Bible Society, 1995).

11. Mitford, p. 50.

12. Ibid.

13. Steve Wiegand and Steve Gibson, "Changing Views on Death Spur New Funeral Traditions," *Sacramento Bee*, April 19, 1999, p. A1.

14. Barley, p. 146–147.

15. Ibid., p. 34.

16. Charles Kuralt, "New Orleans: Charles Kuralt Wanders & Wonders," *Newsday*, December 24, 1995, p. 4.

17. "New Orleans Jazz Funerals," *American Visions*, vol. 13, no. 5, October/November 1998, <http://www.ourpeopletoday.com/views/avs_content/rejoice.htm> (April 12, 1999).

18. Barley, p. 39.

19. Laurence McNamee and Kent Bibble, "Farewells," *Dallas Morning News*, September 7, 1997, p. 9J.

20. *Bartlett's Familiar Quotations*, CD-ROM version (Microsoft Bookshelf, 1991).

21. *Grim Gallery*, The Los Angeles Grim Society, 1997,<http://desperado.scvnet.com/~grim/gallery/fields.html> (April 12,1999).

22. "The Day of the Dead," Palomar College, San Marcos, Calif. 1997, <http://daphne.palomar.edu/muertos/dayofthedead.htm> (April 12, 1999).

23. Paul E. Irion, "Spiritually Speaking," *Journeys: A Newsletter to Help in Bereavement,* Miami Beach, Fla., Hospice Foundation of America, 1995, p. 2.

24. Kenneth J. Doka, "Anniversary Blues—Normal and Difficult," *Journeys: A Newspaper to Help in Bereavement*, Miami Beach, Fla., Hospice Foundation of America, 1995, p. 1.

25. Nicholas Albery, Gil Elliot, and Joseph Elliot, eds., *The Natural Death Handbook* (London, England: The Natural Death Centre, 1995), n.p., 1995 <http://www.worldtrans.org/GIB/natdeath/ndhbook.html> (April 12, 1999).

26. Linda Cunningham, "Grief and the Adolescent," *Teen Age Grief*, Newhall, Calif., Teen Age Grief, Inc., 1996, <http://www.smartlink.net/~tag/grief.html> (April 12, 1999).

27. Ibid.

28. Ibid.

## Chapter 5. Visions of the Afterworld

1. Richard Leakey and Roger Lewin, *Origins Reconsidered: In Search of What Makes Us Human* (New York: Doubleday, 1992), p. 303.

2. Ibid., p. 305.

3. Jim Jenkins, "The Greatness of the Raiders?" *Sacramento Bee*, September 3, 1998, p. D1.

4. Jerome Groopman, M.D., *The Measure of Our Days: New Beginnings at Life's End* (New York: Viking Books, 1997), p. 23.

5. Ibid., pp. 23–24.

6. William Shakespeare, *Macbeth*, Act V, Scene v, Lines 28–29, Jeremy Hylton, ed., *The Complete Works of William Shakespeare*, 1996, <http://www-tech.mit.edu/Shakespeare/table.html> (April 30, 1999).

7. Sheela Pawar, "Basic Synopsis of Process Thought," Center for Process Studies, n.d. <http://www.ctr4process.org> (June 3, 1999).

8. Chaim Stern, ed., *Gates of Prayer: The New Union Prayerbook* (New York: Central Conference of American Rabbis, 1975), p. 626.

9. Groopman, p. 24.

10. Alice K. Turner, *The History of Hell* (New York: Harcourt Brace & Co., 1993), p. 127.

11. Groopman, p. 25.

12. Book of Daniel, 12:2–3, *Holy Bible*, Contemporary English Version (New York: American Bible Society, 1995).

13. Ibid.

14. Ibid.

15. I Corinthians 15: 50–54, *The Bible*, Contemporary English Version, American Bible Society translation (New York: American Bible Society, 1995).

16. Jeffrey Burton Russell, *A History of Heaven: The Singing Silence* (Princeton: Princeton University Press, 1997), p. 15.

17. *The Koran*, E. H. Palmer, trans., in Library of the Future, Series 2nd ed. (Garden Grove, Calif.: World Library, Incorporated, 1991), Chapter IV, par. 10.

18. Ibid., Chapter XXII, par. 15.

19. Ibid.

20. Revelations 14:10–11, *Holy Bible*, Authorized King James Version, Genesis Network, n.d. <http://www.genesis.net.au/reference/bible/kjv> (May 1, 1999).

21. Turner, p. 207.

22. Ibid.

23. Turner, p. 3.

24. Nicholas Albery, Gil Elliot, and Joseph Elliot, eds., *The Natural Death Handbook* (London, England: The Natural

Death Centre, 1995), <http://www.worldtrans.org/GIB/natdeath/ndhbook.html> (April 12, 1999).

25. Ibid.

26. Russell, p. 153.

27. Dante Alighieri, *Inferno*, Canto I, Henry Wadsworth Longfellow, trans., Project Gutenberg text, ed. by Dennis McCarthy, July 1997, n.p., <http://tom.cs.cmu.edu/cgibin/book/lookup?num=1004> (April 12, 1999).

28. Russell, p. 161.

29. Ibid., p. 179.

30. Marilyn Webb, *The Good Death: The New American Search to Reshape the End of Life* (New York: Bantam Books, 1997), p. 243.

## Chapter 6. How Long Is Long Enough?

1. *Concise Columbia Dictionary of Quotations*, CD-ROM version, Microsoft Bookshelf, 1991.

2. Muriel Dobbin, "They're Fat and Happy in New Orleans," *Sacramento Bee*, May 6, 1998, p. E1.

3. Ibid.

4. Ibid.

5. Cynthia Hubert, "She Sacrificed Life for Brief Joy as Mom," *Sacramento Bee*, October 25, 1998, p. A1.

6. Kathryn Doré Perkins, "Health or Longevity: Which Would You Pick?" *Sacramento Bee*, February 4, 1998, p. B1.

7. Natalie Babbitt, *Tuck Everlasting* (New York: Farrar, Straus and Giroux, Sunburst ed., 1985), pp. 62–64.

8. Robert C. W. Ettinger, "The Cryonics Thesis," Cryonics Institute, n.d. <http://www.cryonics.org/reprise.html> (April 12, 1999).

9. Ibid.

10. Ibid.

11. Jeremy Laurance, "Dolly's Team Works on Cystic Fibrosis Cure," *Independent*, June 6, 1997, p. 10.

12. Ben Bova, M.D., *Immortality: How Science is Extending Your Life Span—And Changing the World* (New York: Avon Books, 1998), p. 47.

13. Ibid., p. 49.

14. Ibid., p. 129.

# Further Reading

Byock, Ira, M.D. *Dying Well: Peace and Possibilities at the End of Life*. New York: Riverhead Books, 1998.

Cantor, Norman L. *Advance Directives and the Pursuit of Death With Dignity (Medical Ethics)*. Bloomington, Ind.: Indiana University Press, 1993.

DiGuilio, Robert and Rachel Kranz. *Straight Talk about Death & Dying*. New York: Facts on File, 1995.

Dudley, William, ed. *Death & Dying: Opposing Viewpoints*. San Diego, Calif.: Greenhaven Press, 1992.

Groopman, Jerome, M.D. *The Measure of Our Days: A Spiritual Exploration of Illness*. New York: Viking Penguin, 1998.

Grosshandler-Smith, Janet. *Coping When a Parent Dies*. New York: The Rosen Publishing Group, 1995.

Kearney, Michael. *Mortally Wounded: Stories of Soul Pain, Death & Healing*. New York: Simon & Schuster, 1996.

Kübler-Ross, Elisabeth. *Questions & Answers on Death*. New York: Simon & Schuster, 1997.

Ray, M. Catherine. *I'm Here to Help: A Guide for Caregivers, Hospice Workers, and Volunteers*. New York: Bantam Books, 1997.

Steele, Bill. *After a Loss: Thoughts, Feelings & Behaviors*. New York: P P I Publishing, 1994.

# Internet Addresses

**DeathNET: An international archive specializing in all aspects of death and dying with a sincere respect for every point of view.**
<http://www.rights.org/deathnet/open.html>

**Euthanasia World Directory**
<http://www.finalexit.org>

**GriefNet**
<http://rivendell.org>

**Last Acts: A national coalition to improve care and caring at the end of life.**
<http://www.lastacts.org>

**Myths and Facts About Organ and Tissue Donation**
<http://www.nkfg.org/2/myths.htm>

# Index